THE POETRY OF LÉOPOLD SÉDAR SENGHOR

The Poetry of
Léopold Sédar Senghor

S. OKECHUKWU MEZU

Associate Professor
State University of New York at Buffalo

RUTHERFORD • MADISON • TEANECK
FAIRLEIGH DICKINSON UNIVERSITY PRESS

THE POETRY OF LÉOPOLD SÉDAR SENGHOR.
© 1973 by S. O. Mezu.
First American edition published 1973
by Associated University Presses, Inc.,
Cranbury, New Jersey 08512.

Library of Congress Catalogue Card Number: 73-5107

ISBN 0-8386-1391-8

Printed in the United States of America

Contents

Acknowledgements

▼▼▼▼▼▼▼▼▼▼▼▼▼▼▼▼▼▼▼▼▼▼▼▼▼▼▼▼▼▼▼

FOR PERMISSION to quote poems and extracts of poems acknowledgement is made to the following:

Président L. S. Senghor and Editions du Seuil, Paris, for: 'In Memoriam', 'Nuit de Sine', 'Joal', 'Femme Noire', 'Poème Liminaire', 'A l'Appel de la Race de Saba', 'Méditerranée', 'Au Gouverneur Eboué', 'Camp 1940', 'Lettre à un Prisonnier', 'Prière de Paix', 'Congo', 'A New York', 'Elégie de Minuit', 'Prière des Tirailleurs Sénégalais', 'Luxembourg', 'Au Guelwar', 'Teddungal', 'Messages', 'Assassinats', 'Tyaroye', 'Le Kaya-Magan', 'L'Homme et la Bête', 'L'Absente', 'Tout le Long du Jour', 'Taga de Mbaye Dyôb', 'Aux Soldats Négro-Americains', published in the complete *Poèmes* of Léopold Sédar Senghor (Editions du Seuil, Paris, 1964).

Oxford University Press, London, for English translations of: 'In Memoriam', 'Nuit de Sine', 'Joal', 'Black Woman', 'Preliminary Poem', 'On the Appeal from the Race of Sheba', 'Mediterranean', 'To Governor Eboué', 'Camp 1940', 'Letter to a Prisoner', 'Prayer for Peace', 'Congo', 'New York', and 'Elegy for Midnight' first published in *Léopold Sédar Senghor : Prose and Poetry*, edited and translated by John Reed and Clive Wake (Three Crowns Books, Oxford University Press, London, 1965); 'Prayer for the Tirailleurs of Senegal' 'All Day Long', and 'Man and the Beast' first published in *Selected Poems : Léopold Sédar Senghor* translated by John Reed and Clive Wake (Oxford University Press, London, 1964).

Heinemann Educational Books, London, for English translations of: 'Murders', 'Tyaroye', 'Kaya-Magan', and 'The Absent One' first published in *French African Verse*, translated by John Reed and Clive Wake (African Writers Series 106, Heinemann, London, 1972); 'Taga for Mbaye Dyob', 'To the American Negro Soldiers' first published in *A Book of African Verse*, edited by John Reed and Clive Wake (African Writers Series 8, Heinemann, London, 1964).

We are personally grateful to John Reed and Clive Wake for hitherto unpublished translations into English of the following: 'To the Senegalese Tirailleurs who died for France', 'Luxembourg Gardens 1939', 'To the Guelwar', 'Teddungal', and 'Messages'.

'Et Coetera' by Léon Damas (*Pigments*, Guy Levi Mano, Paris, 1937); 'Song' by Langston Hughes (*The Dreamkeeper and other Poems*, copyright 1932 Alfred A. Knopf, Inc, New York, and renewed 1960 by Langston Hughes. Reprinted by permission of the publisher).

Introduction

▼▼▼▼▼▼▼▼▼▼▼▼▼▼▼▼▼▼▼▼▼▼▼▼▼▼▼▼▼

ON 9 OCTOBER 1906 (some sources indicate 9 August 1906) Léopold Sédar Senghor was born in the small Serere village of Joal in Senegal. Senghor's life, education, development, and career, both literary and political, illustrate the story of the various cultural, social and political changes that affected the black man and his world, and seem to have laid the foundations for the development of black life and culture for generations to come.

Léopold Sédar Senghor was the son of Basile Diogoye Senghor, a man considered fairly well off in his circle. In addition to being a farmer, Basile Diogoye was a cattle-breeder. The Sereres are very hard-working people, and Léopold's father seems to have benefited a great deal from the increase in the export of ground-nuts at the turn of the century. But for Léopold, even at a young age, his ambition lay elsewhere: to become a priest or a teacher. It was to further this objective that he entered the Catholic elementary school in 1913. Up till then, as is common in the Serere matriarchal system, he was greatly attached to his mother, and was known (and to quite a few people is still known) as Sédar Nyilane, the latter being the name of his mother.

Sédar Nyilane was profoundly influenced by this matriarchal system. The mother belonged to the Fulani ethnic group, and most of Senghor's knowledge of local customs and beliefs was imbibed during his frequent visits to his uncle Toko'Waly, the eldest in the maternal line. Apparently his father was not very happy with these frequent trips to the maternal uncle, and quite often had to give his son a sound thrashing to make his point. According to Serere custom, marriage does not imply the foundation of a new family or the absorption of the wife into the family of the man. The woman continues to belong to her people and may return when she becomes widowed or feels herself offended.

Under normal circumstances, at the age of seven Sédar Nyilane would have submitted to the rituals of initiation and apprenticeship in the father's farm. In fact, his initiation was into a new world and culture, that of French civilization. But before then, Sédar had a happy childhood, swimming with the other children, riding on horseback among the coconut plantations, and running around the sandy beaches not far away. When he was not learning about village lore, about medicinal plants and herbs, about birds and animals, about stars and constellations from his maternal uncle Toko'Waly, he used to go to the sandy island of Fadiouth near his native village of Joal, to listen to Marione N'Diaye and her chants of joy and sorrow. (Marône N'Diaye, born around 1890 in Fadiouth, a rival village to Joal, was the best poetess of the area. Senghor has translated some of her poems. She died in 1950.)

Léopold Senghor remembers details of this early childhood with great fondness and striking clarity. In his sixties, these childhood memories are still a source of joy. This contact with nature in its unadulterated form often haunts the Sengalese writer. It is an integral part of his life, so vivid and consoling that he uses the memories as a sort of balm, a refuge in moments of solitude and reflection. This early childhood gave Senghor the material for his lyric poems in Paris. Despite the splendours of political life, perhaps because of the excess of its paraphernalia, Sédar Nyilane comes back to these memories of childhood, already sung in his poems, events evoked several times in his public speeches and television interviewes, images that have become a kind of obsession, romanticized during the years of his absence from Senegal, and because of this process of nostalgic remembrance, taken to be reality itself. Poetic life for Senghor as a result of this becomes a continual quest for the kingdom of childhood, a recovery, a recapture of this idyllic situation where borders between reality and imagination are thin and undefined, where the living villagers and their dead ancestors bathe in the same tree-shaded streams, while in the distance, the owl, crocodiles, cows, mermaids and other creatures fill the air of the setting sun with their respective sounds, concordant, discordant, inviting, frightening, full of awe and splendour.

Naturally – like most of us when, at the age of six or seven, we were put on the road to the neighbourhood school – Sédar Nyilane was not happy when his father, partly to punish him for his frequent and extended visits to his uncle Toko'Waly, decided to 'incarcerate' him in the Catholic mission school at Joal. One can imagine how Sédar felt, dreaming about the beautiful world outside, now beyond his reach, the free farms and woods beyond, the sound of the ocean waves in the distance, the consoling voice of Marône N'Diaye. A year later, he went into the boarding house at Ngasobil, some four miles from Joal, with about seventy other companions. The school was run by Holy Ghost Fathers, who gave the rudiments of education, French grammar, nature study and Latin to the hybrid group of orphans, mulattos and children of notables. Occasionally he came home to see his parents, and during his vacations he used to learn Wolof and a little English from his relations in the Gambia (formerly a British colony).

What was meant to be punishment for the prodigal son turned out to be a unique orientation for a great life of achievement and learning. Senghor wanted to become a priest, and like the other children learned to serve at mass and intone the Gregorian chant. We shall hear later on in his poems echoes of the *Pange Lingua Gloriosi* and the *Pater Noster*. After eight years at Ngasobil, in 1922 Leopold entered the Libermann Junior Seminary at Dakar. It must have been a disorientating experience. From the small elementary school, he moved up to a secondary school. From his small village of Joal where everyone knew his neighbour, he was thrown into Dakar, capital and major port of French West Africa, the main railway station, already in 1922 a city of some 20,000 inhabitants, to a great extent alienated from the traditional customs and sense of hospitality. Senghor here suffered his first spasm of alienation, unable to count again on the advice of his uncle, the tenderness of his mother or even the disciplinary hand of his father. Perhaps the solitary and austere life in the Juniorate provided adequate protection for him. Four years was all he stayed, for around 1926 Father La Touze kindly but firmly told him that he had no vocation. Léopold remained stupefied for a few days, but soon recovered from the setback and now that his first choice of career had failed, turned to his second choice: to become a teacher.

Senghor left the Juniorate and entered the lay secondary school in Dakar, the future Lycée Van Vollenhoven, one of the very first in French West Africa. Not only had the six years in the seminary left an indelible mark on his life, they had also given him solid foundations in the classics: Latin and Greek. He completed his secondary and higher school studies with success, and encouraged and assisted by his Greek master, Pratt, he left in 1928 to continue his studies in Paris with a partial government scholarship. Events were pushing the young Serere student towards new horizons and new heights. Near the end of the summer of 1928, Léopold, the prodigal son, sent to school as a punishment by his father, took the mail-boat *Médie II* in quest of the golden fleece. Those who have experienced it know what it means to leave under such circumstances for a country far away, the mother-country, the home of one's teachers, a country one knows already through history and geography books. He was probably so excited about his final destination that he forgot all about his years in Dakar. Perhaps those days of alienation and disappointment were forgotten. Dakar, at least those days in Dakar, do not feature in his speeches and poems as much as his early years in Joal or the period of time spent in Paris. This is understandable. He was probably very happy to leave Dakar, African yet so foreign, so near to home yet so far away. He was certainly happy to banish from his mind the city that 'rejected' him, a city where the local tropical warmth of body and the imported temperate coldness of heart make the atmosphere unsettling for aliens and natives alike.

It is difficult to say whether Léopold Nyilane would have become a poet if he had remained in Senegal, or if he had not, as it were, been snatched away from home so early in life. Absence makes the heart grow fonder, and distance makes places and persons dearer. Senghor's departure for Paris was perhaps the first indirect step towards a literary career. It happened also that the turn of the century was a momentous period in the history of Africa and the black man. These events made an impression on Senghor, who himself would greatly influence the future course of events affecting Africa and the black man.

In 1902, just before Senghor's birth, Africa was divided up between European powers – England, France, Germany, Portugal, Belgium, Italy, Turkey and Spain – and only three African countries were then independent: Morocco, Ethiopia and Liberia. With the formation of the French West Africa federation in 1904 and French Equatorial Africa in 1910, the era of French interest in Africa really began, and Senegal and Dakar were the centre of French administration. European discovery of African life and culture began just as Africans started to leave the black continent as free men to discover the new world that was Europe, America and Asia. This was an era of mutual discovery.

One can also speak of a veritable Black Renaissance at the turn of the twentieth century. The abolition of the slave trade in the mid-nineteenth century gave the impulse to the movement. Everywhere in the United States were formed organizations for the defence of the black man, a defence Senghor was to push forward later on in his life. In 1897 Alexander Crummel organized in Washington the American Negro Academy, which sought to bring together black intellectuals for the promotion of researches on black problems. In 1900 the Trinidadian lawyer, H. Sylvester Williams, with the support of Bishop Alexander Walters of the African Methodist Episcopal Zion Church, a black separatist church, organized the first pan-African Congress. Senghor himself was to attend the fifth pan-African Congress in Manchester in 1945. Dr Williams Edward B. Du Bois became increasingly active, and his efforts led to the formation of the National Association for the Advancement of Coloured People (N.A.A.C.P.) in 1910. From 1909 the organization propagated its work by publishing the magazine *The Crisis*. This was also the era of Booker T. Washington, the politics of Marcus Garvey, and the 'Back to Africa' movement. Marcus Garvey spoke then of repatriating black Americans to mother Africa. Black separatist and 'protestant' churches were formed to protest against segregation in white churches. These agitations, cultural, political and religious, were manifestations of a new sentiment. Though separated from it by four centuries, one can certainly compare this phenomenon to the European Renaissance, especially in France.

The white Renaissance marked a rupture with the Middle Ages, the current manner of thinking, accepted norms and ideas. It marked a consciousness on the part of the humanist, who discovered that his patrimony stretched back to Greco–Roman times. This self-knowledge did not come suddenly, but was due to a long transition, to separate, disparate movements, and more specifically to the flight of artists and wise men towards the West after the capture of Constantinople by the Turks in 1453. I have no intention of constructing for the twentieth century an absolute homology of events in sixteenth-century Europe. But the similarities are real. In the Black Renaissance, the abolition of the slave trade can be considered as the incident that gave impetus to the movement. The geographical discoveries of the European renaissance enlarged horizons as well as minds. So too the voyages and study trips of Africans in America and in Europe revealed to them a new world, as well as their own world. Black American and West Indian students in Europe had the same experience. These future humanists, black humanists that came before Léopold Senghor, illuminated the face of the black world in search of its independence.

The two renaissances encouraged the spirit of criticism and brought about a rupture with the past. New religious ways were opened up and man desperately sought to liberate himself from the chains of tradition, and once free, to emancipate or help emancipate his brothers. Thus 'scholastic' rigidity gave way in the face of a new liberal humanism; the prejudices of the recent past melted under the influence of new ideas. More important than the awakening of a new consciousness of self, the nation and the race, more important than the rupture of the purely political and religious order, were the new humanism and the love of antiquity called pagan. The black world also wanted to glorify its ancient past, a past long lost but recently rediscovered. At the turn of the century, the black man felt a new urge for self-realization, a new strength coming from new discoveries and the growing knowledge that he had a history and civilization prodigiously rich – the new African civilization soon to be revealed and interpreted. A new optimism appeared everywhere. The awakened black man at the turn of the century recognized that Africa was not so much the continent with culture and civilization, but the source of culture, a living museum of ancient culture and civilizations. Africa was not a *tabula rasa*.

Certainly enormous differences exist between the two renaissances. The Black Renaissance was to rely greatly on the forces of socialism, rationalism and Marxism, as well as on other political and social liberation movements that have become a part of man's experience since the European Renaissance.

Unfortunately, enough attention has not yet been accorded to this movement as a vital and energizing force. It was this that inspired the young black writers of the colonial era in Africa and the West Indies, and above all the young man Léopold Senghor. Senghor has his place in the Black Renaissance movement just as Du Bellay had in the French Renaissance. It would be incorrect to consider Senghor as the pioneer of the Black Renaissance, just as it would be unfair to minimize his great contribution to the movement. Seen in its right perspective, Senghor is rather a product of the Black Renaissance. He is first a product, and then a continuator of the movement, which began when Léopold was born and the apogee of which coincided with the culminating point of his career (in 1960, with the independence of African nations).

Born in Africa when the movement was beginning in the United States, Senghor arrived in Paris when it was gaining ground in Parisian circles. In 1960, both came back to the motherland, to independent Africa.

In his prefaces to *Afrique de l'Ouest, berceau de l'art nègre*, Léopold Senghor regrets the fact that Africa in the mid-twentieth century remains *terra incognita* because the foreigner very often knows only of the external façades, the landscape, animals, plants, monuments and dance. One must learn to forget the zoological gardens for a while: 'To begin with, one must go directly to the Man: I mean what most profoundly reveals Man with authenticity: his art.'

This ignorance Senghor was referring to was more pronounced at the beginning of the century, and the precursors of the Black Renaissance were conscious of the necessity of using the art of the people to explain their feelings. While William Du Bois, Sylvester Williams and others were working in America, a new current was evident in Europe, especially in Paris. The concept of Africa started to change. Maurice Delafosse and Leo Frobenius began their voyages to Africa and started writing their anthropological, then ethnological studies, of the various tribes of Africa and various forms of African culture. The writings of Arthur de Gobineau, for the most part racist, and the works of Gustave Le Bon, laid emphasis on the artistic endowment of the blacks, whom they unfortunately considered to be at the very bottom of the ladder of the human race. Pablo Picasso was moving into a new stage in modern painting. The African influence on his works around 1907 and 1908 is clearly evident. His meeting with Georges Braque in the autumn of 1907 laid the foundation for the Cubist Movement, popularized by Guillaume Apollinaire, who evokes African art in his poem 'Zone'. French artists also made their contribution to the recognition of African art and culture. Gradually literature of the blacks increased and appreciation of black art and culture grew, from day to day and from article to article.

This gave rise to more literary works like the novel of René Maran, a West Indian, who published *Batouala, véritable roman nègre*, which won for him the 1921 Prix Goncourt, in Paris. There were Congresses on African problems and culture everywhere – London, Brussels, Lisbon and New York. Other works followed. André Gide, himself influenced by this vogue, wrote an account of his travels in Africa, *Voyage au Congo*, and *Retour du Tchad*. In 1928 Dr Jean Price-Mars published his work *Ainsi parla l'Oncle*. A colleague of Senghor's, Léon Damas, has acknowledged that the works of Jean Price-Mars were one of the points of departure and sources of inspiration for future black writers, poets, novelists and historians of the Paris group that included Senghor.

This was the general climate when Senghor arrived in Paris in October 1928. These external forces would only serve to sharpen his own sensitivity, and reveal the artist that was already budding in him. These forces would also influence the nature of his writing, colour his vision and his vocabulary to create the unique and novel nature of his poetry. Thus he was able to present to a French audience, in French, a new message with powerful content.

Léopold Senghor, during his days at the Lycée Louis le Grand with co-students like Georges Pompidou, would learn to admire French writers like Baudelaire, Rimbaud, Claudel and Maurice Barrès. Surprisingly, Senghor does not appear to have been influenced by André Malraux. Rimbaud does not seem to have influenced his writing either. Senghor's is a quiet personality, conformist rather than revolutionary, religious rather than demoniac. His admiration of Baudelaire seems to have centred around the exotic themes in the works of the poet. As a black man, he could probably not help being impressed by Baudelaire's celebration of Jeanne Duval, the black and diabolic beauty, the tropical mermaid. Claudel seems to have been a strong influence on Senghor's metre and sentiments. Long after the Lycée days, one can see traces of Claudelian verse forms and metre, and even vocabulary, in Senghor's poetry. Besides coming under the influence of the great French masters and the surrealist movement then current in France, Senghor met other black students, especially Aimé Césaire from Martinique, a little younger than Senghor, but definitely bolder and more forceful in his revolutionary fervour and zeal, not unfortunately tempered by practical experience and concerete action.

It was through Aimé Césaire and other black students in Paris that Senghor suddenly discovered his blackness, a feeling nurtured and sharpened by the current of racism then sweeping Europe. There was the Italian invasion of Ethiopia, the civil war in Spain, the anti-Machado struggles in Cuba, the suppression of the Jews in Germany. Faced with the insecurity of the white system of values, Senghor and his colleagues started to look into themselves, into African 'primitive' cultures and civilizations, for new solutions and avenues to happiness and peace of mind. They were not alone in this search. In Europe the surrealist movement led by André Breton was already trying to make use of the discoveries of Freud in psychoanalysis to bring the individual back to his hidden and unconscious self. Surrealism was trying to go back to the 'primitive' society, the earthly paradise, for comfort and solace in a highly rationalistic world pioneered by Descartes and crystallized by Bergson, who assigned new horizons and possibilities to the intelligence in the solving of human problems.

To propagate these new ideas, the blacks in Paris led by Paullete Nardal, a West Indian, and Dr Leo Sajous, started the publication of the magazine *La revue du monde noir*, which in addition to encouraging new writing popularized the works of black American authors. Its professed motto was to give the opportunity to black intellectuals and their friends of publishing artistic, literary and scientific works. It planned to propagate matters of particular interest to black civilization, and to tell of the riches of Africa. It planned to create a feeling of oneness without distinction of nationality, an intellectual and moral union between all blacks in order to make them better able to defend and embellish their civilization.

This would eventually be the unadvertised motto of Léopold Senghor: the defence and celebration of the black civilization – *la défense et illustration de la civilisation noire*. Senghor refers to this theme at least three times in his speeches and lectures. There have been previous instances of such efforts in literary history. There is the case (already quoted) of Du Bellay and the Pléiade during the French Renaissance. Closer to our time, there was the effort of a group of Negro writers in Harlem around 1920 to defend and propogate the black heritage. Some of them visited Paris at this period, and Senghor learned about several others either through the *Revue du monde noir* or through the wide-ranging anthology of Alain Locke, *The New Negro*, published in 1925. There were selections from Dunbar, Du Bois, Jean Toomer, Zora Neale Hurston, Countee Cullen, Claude McKay, James Weldon Johnson, Langston Hughes, Anna Bontemps, Jessie Fauset, Franklin Frazier, Melville Herskovitts, Walter White, Eric Walrond and Rudolph Fisher.

It is not certain to what extent these readings influenced the works of the budding poet Senghor. But he appears to have picked up a new 'revolutionary' vocabulary from his black brothers from America. In Countee Cullen, Senghor saw a new vocabulary exceptionally rare in the Western literature that he had read in Latin, Greek and French. In his works Countee Cullen speaks of 'regal black', 'strong bronze men', 'jungle star', 'jungle track', 'copper sun'. For centuries, both royalty and the sun had always been represented as 'white'. In the works of Langston Hughes and James Weldon Johnson, Senghor heard chants of the black woman, black beauty, the black motherland. Darkness takes possession of the poetic world of these authors. Often, though, it is not the darkness of sorrow, symbol of suffering and the antithesis of life itself. It is the darkness that gives rise to light, the veritable sign and symbol of life. One can imagine the young Léopold Senghor sitting down at the head of his bed, hands to his forehead, in the poorly lit room of the Fondation Deutsche de la Meurthe, reading the prophetic works of Langston Hughes, with a mixture of pride and hope: words that appeared in the Harlem publication *Fire*, a magazine that did not live to see a second issue, for financial reasons.

> We younger Negro artists who create now intend to express our indi-
> vidual darkskinned selves without fear or shame. If white people are
> pleased, we are glad. If they are not, it doesn't matter . . . If colored people

are pleased, we are glad. If they are not, their displeasure doesn't matter either.[1]

One can imagine Senghor reading the passage over and over again, thinking about the history of the black people over the centuries, and the tremendous changes that had taken place during his own lifetime. One can imagine him taking up his pen to pour forth his joy and sorrow – mostly sorrow in the land of exile that was Paris, regretting the black land far away, the black rays of the black sun, the black beauty of the black woman, the dark life with black comrades now so far away. . . .

[1] Langston Hughes, 'The Twenties: Harlem and its Negritude', *Africa Forum* (New York), vol. I, no. 4, Spring 1966, p. 19.

Chants d'Ombre

Chants d'Ombre

▼▼▼▼▼▼▼▼▼▼▼▼▼▼▼▼▼▼▼▼▼▼▼▼▼▼▼▼▼▼▼▼

THOSE WHO have lived abroad, away from their own countries, need not be told what alienation means. This feeling of estrangement from the environment, from the people around, from the society we live in, the culture we find ourselves in, is common in contemporary urban and industrial society. It does not all come suddenly. In America, it is said that the foreign student the first year adores everything he sees; the second year, he becomes a little critical; the third year of his stay, when he has begun to acquire the basic things America has to offer, he begins to hate all around him and wants to go back to his beautiful peasant homeland. His real appreciation of American culture only comes in retrospect, after he has been away from it for a while. The story is the same of every country. Senghor must have experienced the same feelings, gone through the same stages of admiration, judgement and reaction during his long stay in Paris. This process of alienation explains why in his first volume of poetry, Senghor has little or nothing to tell us about the beauty of Paris. These poems were written during the third stage of his stay away from home. His view of Paris is negative. He seems to hate – this word is perhaps too strong – he appears not to like very much what he sees around him. By the time he started writing his first poems, he had gone beyond the stage of mere criticism. It had become condemnation. The student in exile is about ready to go home. He wants to go back to his quiet peasant village. He wants to leave Paris behind, with all its sophistication, its development and its culture.

There are examples of this in all literature. The tendency is always to idealize the object that is far away. The best lines of love poetry are often written in praise or honour of loves that have refused to requite the lover, or for objects that are beyond reach, far beyond the possibility of immediate possession. Du Bellay's great patriotic poems were not written in France but in Rome.

> Je me promène seul sur la rive latine
> La France regrettant, et regrettant encor
> Mes antiques amis, mon plus riche trésor,
> Et le plaisant séjour de ma terre angevine.
> Je regrette les bois, et les champs blondissans,
> Les vignes, les jardins, et les prez verdissans
> Que mon fleuve traverse.

[Alone I stroll along the Roman bank,
Missing France, and missing even more
My friends of old, my richest treasure,
And the pleasant abode of my Angevine land.
How I miss the woods, the blooming fields,
The vines, the gardens and meadows green,
Through which flow my river.]

Senghor, after missing his homeland and returning there, was to revisit Paris. It was only then that he saw the glorious city in its right perspective. Then he had nothing but words of love and songs of praise for Lutèce, *la ville des lumières*. With this background in mind, the reader can then open the first volume of Senghor's poetry, *Chants d'Ombre*, poems written mostly between 1930 and 1939, but published after the war in 1945 when the poet was almost forty years old.

The first poem in the collection, but not necessarily the first to be composed, is 'In Memoriam':

C'est Dimanche
J'ai peur de la foule de mes semblables au visage de pierre
De ma tour de verre qu'habitent les migraines, les Ancêtres impatients
Je contemple toits et collines dans la brume
Dans la paix – les cheminées sont graves et nues.

[Sunday.
The crowding stony faces of my fellows make me afraid.
Out of my tower of glass haunted by headaches and my restless Ancestors
I watch the roofs and hills wrapped in mist
Wrapped in peace . . . the chimneys are heavy and stark.]

There are several interesting elements in this poem, elements that recur in other poems in the collection. The title itself takes us back to the young Léopold at Ngasobil, studying his Latin, serving mass, back to the young man at the lycée going to mass every morning and chanting the psalms. If the poem underscores his religious training, it betrays also the great change going on in his mind. Despite the biblical cadence of the verses, a cadence that reminds the aware reader of Paul Claudel, he appears to be questioning the very principles of the religion by which he had lived since his childhood. This is an aspect of the negation of the culture of his milieu. Like a stranger, the poet looks out from the window across the fog at the crowd of worshippers in their Sunday best. He is able to see the crowds because he is no longer a part of it. A physical as well as a psychological distance separates him from them. He does not belong to the crowd with faces stiff like stone. The poet analyses this crowd, this group, as if it were an object of scientific investigation. From his observatory in his Parisian room, he is able to dissect these objects of flesh and blood spread out on the geometrically converging lines that form the streets of Paris. The poet will have nothing to do with this world of stone, soulless and full of guile. For comfort and solace, his mind wanders to his homeland, to the banks of the rivers Gambia and Saloum.

Twenty years later, though, the poet was to revisit Paris and the places of his stay in the French capital – the Sorbonne, the museums, the palaces. The sight of the city then evoked memories suppressed by the alienation of those early days. Though speaking in prose, he described the capital with words as beautiful and charming as those of his most lyrical poems about Joal and his homeland, written while he was in Paris as a student. A typical example of this is his speech before the Parisian Municipal Council in 1961:

> I first knew the streets of Paris as an inquisitive tourist. Not so much Paris by night as the capital that has so much to offer during the day. Ah! that light that the smoke from factories never succeeds in tarnishing. Blond, blue, grey according to the season, the day, the hour, it remains always delicate and nuanced, illuminating trees and stones, animating everything with that spirit particular to Paris.
>
> Paris is not limited to the bounds of the outer boulevards. The Ile de France is like a crown, the woods of Chevreuse and Ermenonville, the forests of Chantilly and Montmorency, the valleys of the Oise, Marne and Seine, all these landscapes bask under the same sun and light, immortalized by the greatest of painters. The smile of May and the splendour of September there hymn the sweetness of life.
>
> Yes, for me, Paris is first of all this, a city – a symbol of stones – looking out on a harmonious countryside of rivers, flowers, forests, hills. A countryside which portrays a soul befitting man. And the whole thing is illuminated by the light of the Spirit.[1]

Until Paris is revisited, the student living in academic exile still has a long way to go in poetic quest for the motherland. In exile, everything is idealized, rivers, fields, friends, home and gardens. Senghor missed all these in Paris. He very successfully conjures up this image of the eternal search in his poem 'Tout le long du jour'.

Tout le long du jour, sur les longs rails étroits . . .
Tout le long du jour, tout le long de la ligne . . .
Tout le long du jour, durement secoué sur les bancs du train de féraille et
    poussif et poussiéreux,
Me voici cherchant l'oubli de l'Europe au coeur pastoral du Sine[2]

[1] Senghor, *Liberté* I, pp. 312–13.
[2] Sine – the home region of Léopold Senghor.

[All day long along the long straight rails . . .
All day long, all along the line . . .
All day long, roughly shaken on the benches of the clanking, dust-covered
   wheezing, antique train
I come seeking to forget about Europe in the pastoral heart of Sine.]

The days seem interminable, the months, the years, the stay abroad seems
interminable as the poet in 'exile' relives moments spent in favourite childhood haunts at Cayor and Baol, the chattering coloured girls coming out of
the school gate like birds flying out of a cage. Abroad, meanwhile, solitude
redoubles the length of the day, and the solitude is felt even more because of
the hostile environment. Senghor's choice of vowels here is worthy of note.
The sounds 'tout', 'long', 'jour', repeated, taken up again, convey not only the
image of lassitude but the depth of the longing. The rhythm suggests that the
action in question is a daily routine, the poet's daily search for a way to escape
the confines of Europe by thinking of the beauty of his homeland. It is not
surprising that this poem should be followed by 'Nuit de Sine', which
celebrates the beauty of the tropical night, not just the stars and countryside
but the human warmth, the togetherness, the light touch of life, in a quiet
village, lost to modern civilization but happier because of this Eden-like
purity:

Femme pôse sur mon front tes mains balsamiques, tes mains douces plus
   que
   fourrure.
Là-haut les palmes balancées qui bruissent dans la haute brise nocturne
A peine. Pas même la chanson de nourrice.
Qu'il berce, le silence rythmé.
Ecoutons son chant, écoutons battre notre sang sombre, écoutons
Battre le pouls profond de l'Afrique dans la brume des villages perdus.
Voici que décline la lune lasse vers son lit de mer étale
Voici que s'assoupissent les éclats de rire, que les conteurs eux-mêmes
Dodelinent de la tête comme l'enfant sur le dos de mère
Voici que les pieds des danseurs s'alourdissent, que s'alourdit la langue
   des choeurs alternés.

[Woman, lay on my forehead your perfumed hands, hands softer than fur.
Above, the swaying palm trees rustle in the high night breeze
Hardly at all. No lullaby even.
The rhythmic silence cradles us.
Listen to its song, listen to our dark blood beat, listen
To the deep pulse of Africa beating in the mist of forgotten villages.

See the tired moon comes down to her bed on the slack sea
The laughter grows weary, the story-tellers even
Are nodding their heads like a child on the back of its mother
The feet of the dancers grow heavy, and heavy the voice of the answering
    choirs.]

Marcel Proust in his *Temps Retrouvé* discusses the greatness of literature as a
form of art, the only one that can capture the other forms of artistic expression
– painting, music, even drama. Senghor has a way, when he is in the mood, of
capturing a variety of images – descriptive, sensuous, psychological. We hear
the laughter, the voices of story-tellers, we see the receding moon, the
blinking stars, the hills beyond. Closer still we see men, women and children
living their normal lives at the close of a long, hard day. Closer still, we can
feel the very pulse of the heart, as the flow of blood decreases and increases
following the rhythm and tenor of the story and the events of the evening.
Here it is not enough to speak of a poet in exile recalling events of childhood.
True enough, exile provides the mood; and the search for the palace of
childhood supplies the vehicle. But once through these series of symbols and
images the poet and his reader are transported into the kingdom of infancy,
extraneous chains are cut off as the poet loses himself and his reader in
this simple, almost paradisiacal world. Together, we listen to the voices
from beyond:

Ecoutons la voix des Ancêtres d'Elissa. Comme nous exilés
Ils n'ont pas voulu mourir, que se perdît par les sables leur torrent séminal
Que j'écoute, dans la case enfumée que visite un reflet d'âmes propices
Ma tête sur ton sein chaud comme un dang au sortir du feu et fumant
Que je respire l'odeur de nos Morts, que je recueille et redise leur voix
    vivante, que j'apprenne à
Vivre avant de descendre, au-delà du plongeur, dans les hautes profondeurs
    du sommeil.

[Listen to the voice of the ancients of Elissa. Exiled like us
They have never wanted to die, to let the torrent of their seed be lost in the
    sands.
Let me listen in the smoky hut where there comes a glimpse of the friendly
    spirits
My head on your bosom warm like a *dang* smoking from the fire,
Let me breathe the smell of our Dead, gather and speak out again their
    living voice, learn to
Live before I go down, deeper than the diver, into the high profundities
    of sleep.]

Yet in spite of the poet's desire, his deep wish to live to enjoy the present before the eternal journey to the world beyond, the student in exile cannot quite forget that he is in a strange land. Memories invade the mind, memories of childhood flood over his mind as incidents and events, situations and objects; smells and sounds assail his senses. The poem in question is 'Joal'. Joal means a lot to Senghor. It is his home, his cherished home in spite of years of travel abroad. Joal is his native village. It is the one place in life he knows inside out, the one place he can call his own. He knew everyone there and they knew him. The poem starts with the single word: 'Joal!' The exclamation mark there is like a tear telling a story the mind cannot quite conjure up or the tongue verbalize. 'I remember,' he continues:

Je me rappelle les signares[1] à l'ombre verte des vérandas

Les signares aux yeux surréels comme un clair de lune sur la grève.

Je me rappelle les fastes du Couchant
Où Koumba N'Dofène[2] voulait faire tailler son manteau royal.

Je me rappelle les festins funèbres fumant du sang des troupeaux égorgés
Du bruit des querelles, des rhapsodies des griots[3]

Je me rappelle les voix païennes rythmant le *Tantum Ergo,*
Et les processions et les palmes et les arcs de triomphe.

Je me rappelle la danse des filles nubiles
Les choeurs de lutte – oh! la danse finale des jeunes hommes, buste
Penché élancé, et le pur cri d'amour des femmes – *Kor Siga!*[4]

Je me rappelle, je me rappelle . . .
Ma tête rythmant
Quelle marche lasse le long des jours d'Europe où parfois
Apparaît un jazz orphelin qui sanglote sanglote sanglote.

[I remember the *signares* in the green shadow of the verandas
Signares with eyes surreal as moonlight on the beach.
I remember the pomps of sunset
That Kumba N'Dofene wanted cut to make his royal cloak.

I remember the funeral feasts, smoking with the blood of slaughtered
    cattle
With the noise of quarrels and the *griot's* rhapsodies.

[1] Ladies of great honour.
[2] The king of Sine, home region of Senghor.
[3] Griot – courtier, poet.
[4] The son of Siga.

I remember pagan rhythmic singing of the *Tantum Ergo*
And processions and palms and triumphal arches.
I remember the dance of the girls who are ready for marriage

The choruses at the wrestling ... oh! the young men in the final dance bodies
Bent forward, slender and the women's pure shout of love ... *Kor Siga*!

I remember, I remember ...
In my head the rhythm of the tramp tramp
So wearily down the days of Europe where there comes,
Now and then a little orphaned jazz that goes sobbing, sobbing, sobbing.]

'Joal' is easily one of the most beautiful poems created by Senghor, and a good deal has been written and will be written about practically every line of this poem. It may not be out of place here to comment on his use of punctuation. Mostly after the symbolist era, punctuation in poetry became very scanty, as poets used indentation, capitals, visual images, type disposition and even blank lines and pages, as in the case of Mallarmé, to convey an inner, unexpressed and perhaps inexplicable meaning. Senghor is definitely very miserly with punctuation marks, especially commas. But his use in this poem of the exclamation mark is exceptionally effective. There are three in the poem we are considering.

> Joal!
> – oh! la danse finale des jeunes hommes ...
> – *Kor Siga*!

The first is a pensive exclamation that sets the entire chain of thoughts going. It is reflective. It is not really a cry of surprise, of fear or horror. It is one of sorrow, of tears, and of habit. Remembrance of the events of childhood for a while clears up this sorrow. In the poem, the poet seems to be talking to himself or to an *alter ego*. He remembers and recounts. The rhythm increases and the mood lightens as he names all the visions that come before his mind. There is a panting movement as if he wants to name them all at once. All of a sudden, the chain is broken again by sorrow, by an exceptionally nostalgic remembrance – *la danse finale des jeunes hommes*. The next line abolishes all traces of sorrow again as the poem reaches its climax – masculine, virile, vigorous, joyful – with *Kor Siga*, the son of Siga.

Wrestling is extremely popular in Senegal. This wrestling is completely different from the TV wrestling in European countries. Matches are not rigged, and are still used to test strength and masculinity. Among the Wolofs, *lambe*, 'wrestling', means to 'test', to 'measure strength'. It is a means of putting to the test the virility and vigour of young men. This custom is found in other

parts of Africa, though it is gradually falling into desuetude. The first stage of
the wrestling, the *mbapatte*, makes it possible for villages to choose those who
will carry the banners of the community on the regional or national level.

To incite the wrestlers to a match, women and children, and particularly
the sisters of the combatants, try to prick the pride of the participants by
singing their favourite wrestling songs. They chant the praises of their
champion, and try to discourage his adversary. 'Give up your boasting,' they
say, 'only women babble. If it were a question of beauty, we ourselves would
be in the ring, and there would win.' In the background there are the drums,
the choruses; fever mounts, emotions rise, the wrestlers confront one another
like two famished tigers, to build or mar their reputation, to vindicate the
honour or sign the shame of their families, villages and region. Between the
First and the Second World Wars, the Lebou called Pathé Diop was one of the
greatest wrestlers Senegal had ever seen. Senghor was probably thinking of
him when he wrote these words.

The poet at this point has a right to smile and shake his head as his mind
begins to rove again: 'je me rappelle, je me rappelle . . .' Certainly, Senghor
could remember a thousand and one things he could describe with the same
precision, feeling and nostalgia. He appears to come to the conclusion that it
is a heart-rending exercise for an exile so many miles and faces away from his
people. So he abandons the project, leaving it suspended as it were, with a view
to picking it up again at a more favourable time. The days of regret have not
ended. But never again will they be captured with the same simplicity,
naturalness, and spontaneity. This poem almost seems to mark the end of pure
poetic nostalgia in Senghor's writing, the era when he wrote not for publication but for catharsis. In *Chants d'Ombre* he would write other beautiful poems,
but they were to be about the black woman, or the Negro mask; dedicated to
Pablo Picasso or Aimé Césaire or René Maran, the poems condemn the
westernization of the black continent and extol the virtues of blackness; they
talk about death and about blues and jazz, about visits and travels, departures
and arrivals, especially the return of the prodigal son, but they never again
recapture the swanlike beauty and Eden-like simplicity of 'Joal'. Certainly
they have their own form of beauty, their own poetic message, their symbols
and images, their share of cadential and rhythmic innovation. They are
different, but not really superior to 'Joal', for the poem is in a class of its
own.

By far the most often cited poem of Senghor is his classic *Femme noire*.
The popularity of this poem is probably partly due to its ideological content,
its glorification of the black woman.

Certainly, Senghor was not a pioneer in this regard. Charles Baudelaire
before him had chanted the beauties of Jeanne Duval, the coloured prostitute
who inspired several of his poems. But in Baudelaire's work, Jeanne Duval

represented sin, temptation, evil, spleen, in spite of the beauty attached to her memory. This devilish memory was even more set apart in the work of Baudelaire by his veneration of Madame Sabatier, a white woman, whom he never physically possessed but adored no less than Jeanne Duval. For Baudelaire, Madame Sabatier represented the good, the beautiful, the angelic side of life. No real racist connotations should be attached to this aspect of Baudelaire. It is part and parcel of the ambivalence in his life, his twin tendencies towards good and evil, an ambivalence that explains the antithetical titles of his works: *Fleurs du Mal* (Flowers of Evil) and *Spleen et Idéal*. It is therefore a welcome change to see the beauty of a black woman celebrated for its own sake, because of her blackness.

> Femme nue, femme noire
> Vêtue de ta couleur qui est vie, de ta forme qui est beauté!
> J'ai grandi à ton ombre; la douceur de tes mains bandait mes yeux. . . .

> Femme nue, femme obscure
> Fruit mûr à la chair ferme, sombres extases du vin noir, bouche qui fais
> lyrique ma bouche

> [Naked woman, black woman
> Clothed with your colour which is life, with your form which is beauty!
> In your shadow I have grown up; the gentleness of your hands was laid
> over my eyes. . . .

> Naked woman, dark woman
> Firm-fleshed ripe fruit, sombre raptures of black wine, mouth making
> lyrical my mouth]

This is definitely a revolutionary poem within the context of Africa around 1936. For more than three thousand years the white man, European man, had chanted the beauty of the white woman: Dante, Boccaccio, Spenser, and in recent times poets such as Paul Éluard and William Butler Yeats. Certainly with no thoughts of racism – for they were innocently recording their own experiences – they praised without restraint the beauty of the white woman, her white and elegant hands, the whiteness of her face, radiant as the sun, dazzling as the moon. Beauty and whiteness and cleanliness almost became synonymous. Even Rimbaud in his famous poem 'Voyelles' associated E with whiteness, candour, radiance, glory. A was associated with blackness, a putrefying smell and the buzzing of flies. It was therefore a welcome change, this glorification of the black woman because of the colour of her skin.

The poem was undoubtedly revolutionary for its time, but the way had been opened up by the black American writers at the beginning of the century, and

in a way, Léopold Senghor was only continuing a tradition initiated by
Langston Hughes, Claude McKay, Countee Cullen and the rest of the poets
of the Black Renaissance period. Senghor more than anyone else recognizes
this debt to the American writers. Speaking about American Negro poetry,
Senghor said in 1950:

> The message of McKay finally came across. More than the mere accept-
> ance of a fact was the development among the poets of today of pride in
> their race. The latter believe that along with the new values, it brings the
> life-blood of spring that will regenerate American civilization. And they
> have an entirely unique cult made up of respect and love, of desire and
> adoration, for the *black woman*, symbolized by negritude. For women are,
> more so than men, sensitive to the mysterious currents of life and of the
> cosmos, open to the joys and sweetness of life.

One need only quote the poem of Langston Hughes: 'Song':

> Lovely, dark, and lonely one,
> Bare your bosom to the sun,
> Do not be afraid of light
> You who are a child of night.
>
> Open wide your arms to life,
> Whirl in the wind of pain and strife,
> Face the wall with the dark closed gate,
> Beat with bare, brown fists
> And wait.

Other black American poets, like Gwendolyn Bennet and Frank Marshall,
had also sung of this beauty: black and fair, fair because it is black, beautiful
because it is the colour of night.

One interesting aspect of Senghor's poem is that it does not seem to be
addressed to any particular woman. He speaks of the black woman in a
generic sense. Hence the poem has a somewhat intellectual flavour. One can
also see the influence of the European surrealist poets, who used the litany
technique extensively. Surrealism was very popular about the time when the
poem was probably written. In form and structure, it reminds one of the
poems, at least certain poems, of Paul Éluard and André Breton. The technique of the litany is adopted, as in the litany of the Virgin Mary, in order to
enumerate the many and varied attributes of the object of love and veneration.
Without going into detail one could draw an analogy with 'L'union libre' of
André Breton. Just as in the Catholic litany of the Virgin, the Mother of

Christ is described as 'the gate of heaven', 'morning star', 'star of David' 'Tower of Ivory', 'golden gate', so in the poem 'Femme noire', the following expressions are seen:

> Femme nue
> Femme noire
> Femme obscure,
> Fruit mûr à la chair ferme
> Sombres extases du vin noir
> Bouche qui fais lyrique ma bouche
> Savane aux horizons purs
> Savane qui frémis aux caresses ferventes du Vent d'Est
> Tamtam sculpté
> Tamtam tendu
> Huile que ne ride nul souffle
> Huile calme aux flancs de l'athlète
> Gazelle aux attaches célestes
> Délices des jeux de l'esprit
> Femme nue
> Femme noire. . . .

This is the surrealist ideal, which seeks to abstract in an infinite number of ways, through an infinite number of variations and nuances, the various facets of the object of adoration. One does not have to strain a great deal to see the influence of the poem 'L'union libre' on Senghor's creation of another aesthetic love. André Breton writes thus:

> Ma femme à la chevelure de feu de bois
> Aux pensées d'éclairs de chaleur
> A la taille de sablier
> Ma femme à la taille de loutre entre les dents du tigre
> Ma femme à la bouche de cocarde et de bouquet d'étoiles de dernière
>   grandeur
> Aux dents d'empreintes de souris blanches sur la terre blanche
> A la langue d'ambre et de verre frotté
> Ma femme à la langue d'hostie poignardée . . .

Abstraction appears dominant in the poem of Senghor. One does not sense the suffering of a poet that feels real love, definable love for a woman loved but far away. The 'femme noire' of Léopold Senghor is the product of a dream in exile. Owing to this absence of an individual, owing to the absence of a sense of direction, one gets the impression that the poet, like Spenser, like Ronsard, wants to fix in time and space the passing beauty, the fading beauty of a black 'Helen'. The form which the poet wants to fix for future generations is perhaps not so much the beauty of a black woman before her physical death but rather that of a certain idea of a black woman before her disappearance *dans un monde métis*, in a world of mixed races:

> Femme nue, femme noire
> Je chante ta beauté qui passe, forme que je fixe dans l'Éternel
> Avant que le Destin jaloux ne te réduise en cendres pour nourrir les racines de la vie.

> [Naked woman, black woman,
> I sing your beauty that passes, the form that I fix in the Eternal,
> Before jealous Fate turn you to ashes to feed the roots of life.]

There is, in a way, a racist flavour in this poem. This is perhaps what led Mustapha Bal to write that singing about, and paying homage to, woman is a good thing in itself, but that the chances are the blacks are not amongst the first to do this. Bal continues in this vein:

> Singing the praises of the black woman, emphasizing her quality of blackness, is poetic and revolutionary in so far as it marks a moment of a certain consciousness that must be left behind. Negro–African poetry, if it wants to achieve significance, must go beyond this infantile stage: that of conferring a virtue on the black man simply because the white man has abused him.[1]

Mustapha Bal here raises the question of reverse racism in black literature. Some critics have frequently accused black poets of the generation of Senghor for being racist during at least a certain period of their careers. Gerald Moore in his book *Seven African Writers* argues that this form of racism is 'as intolerant and arrogant' as any other, and at its worst could lead to the writing of defiant nonsense. But he does credit it with the power of unlocking the talents of the poet and providing a vehicle for his passion, energy and conviction.[2] Senghor's poem should be classified in the latter category.

It is a fact though that some black writers of Senghor's generation did go through a phase of seeing nothing but goodness in the black race. In 1948 Jean-Paul Sartre defined this phenomenon as an 'anti-racist racism' in his

---

[1] Mustapha Bal, 'L'homme noir dans la poésie', *Pensée* no. 103, mai–juin 1962, p. 25.
[2] Gerald Moore, *Seven African Writers* (Oxford University Press, London, 1962) p. xix.

celebrated and classic preface to Senghor's *Anthologie de la nouvelle poésie nègre et malgache*. Sartre, true to his philosophy, does not condemn this phenomenon but merely analyses it, trying at the same time to suggest its origin and what future if any it has: In 'Orphée noir', Sartre writes:

> Behold black men, erect, looking at us white people, and I invite you to feel as I have felt the sensation of being dissected by looks. The white man has enjoyed for a thousand years the privilege of seeing without being looked at. . . . A black poet, without even caring how whites feel, whispers to the woman he loves:
>
> > 'Naked woman, black woman
> > Clothed with your colour which is life . . .
> > Naked woman, dark woman
> > Firm-fleshed ripe fruit, sombre raptures of black wine. . . .'
>
> and our whiteness appears like a deathly pale and strange varnish that prevents our skin from breathing, swaddling-clothes shabby at the elbows and the knees under which, if we could remove it, would appear the real human flesh, flesh the colour of dark wine.[1]

[1] Jean-Paul Sartre, 'Orphée noir', preface to *Anthologie de la nouvelle poésie nègre et malgache*, ed. Léopold Sédar Senghor (Presses Universitaires de France, Paris 1948) pp. ix–x.

Hosties Noires

Hosties Noires

▼▼▼▼▼▼▼▼▼▼▼▼▼▼▼▼▼▼▼▼▼▼▼▼▼▼▼▼▼▼

THERE IS a perceptible change in style and theme in the volume *Hosties noires*, published in 1948 but mostly written during the Second World War. Here the reader no longer sees reminiscences of a young man by the fireside, as in *Chants d'Ombre*, but songs of action and strife, of war and peace, of suffering and hope. The first poem, simply called 'Poème Liminaire', is dedicated to Léon Gontrin Damas, himself a fighter who wrote the controversial works *Pigment* and *Retour de Guyanne*, and who generally asked black people, Africans in particular, not to fight in a European war, to liberate those very people who enslaved their forefathers and who continued to colonize them in Africa. At his call, the people of the Ivory Coast refused to be conscripted into the French Army. Therefore, Senghor's dedication of his poem to Damas has a double meaning. Firstly, he recognizes the fighter-friend, Léon Damas, his companion during their days in Paris. Secondly, he draws a sharp line between his views and those of Damas, the rebel, the non-conformist preaching revolt against French authority.

Here, Damas, far from being pacifist, is very bellicose. He is direct in his approach, almost brutal in his challenge of authority. He lacks refinement, if such a word can correctly be applied to literature. He indulges in neither euphemisms nor vague generalizations. He goes to the point without nuances, irony, or innuendos. Senghor's dedication of the 'Poème Liminaire' to Damas is less a mark of friendship and more a distancing of his views from those of the writer from Guadeloupe. The Senegalese fighters dying in foreign lands are not heroes in the eyes of Damas. Senghor views them very differently. They are black victims in a white war, but their sacrifice is viewed as being meaningful, and for the good not only of France but of mankind:

Vous Tirailleurs Sénégalais, mes frères noirs à la main chaude sous la
  glace et la mort
Qui pourra vous chanter si ce n'est votre frère d'armes, votre frère de sang?

Je ne laisserai pas la parole aux ministres, et pas aux généraux
Je ne laissera pas – non! – les louanges de mépris vous enterrer furtivement.
Vous n'êtes pas des pauvres aux poches vides sans honneur
Mais je déchirerai les rires *banania* sur tous les murs de France.

[You, *tirailleurs* of Senegal, black brothers, warm-handed under ice and
death,
Who but I should sing of you, your brother in arms, in blood?

I will not leave the speeches to ministers nor to generals
I will not leave you to be buried darkly with a little contemptuous praise.
You are not poor with nothing in your pockets without honour
I will tear down the *banania* smiles from every wall in France.]

Senghor in *Hosties Noires* is therefore going to sing the glory of those forgotten black Africans who fought in a white war. He is singing as one who took
part in the campaign as well. France was not particularly grateful to the
Senegalese soldiers who fought for her during the First World War, and this
was the subject of a few books and several articles. There was discrimination
in the army between the 'natives' and the French soldiers, just as was the case
even in the American Army, between the whites and blacks. It is with this
background of emotion and pride that the Senegalese poet sets out to com-
memorate the glory of his comrades, ignored by politicians. When he writes:
'Je ne laisserai pas – non! – les louanges de mépris vous enterrer furtivement. . . .' could the poet really be thinking of the sarcastic remarks of some
poets like Leon Damas, disparaging certain 'honours' that seem to bury the
heroism of the Trailleurs Sénégalais? But the poem is far from being a polemic.
It is a lyric cry of a native son on behalf of his comrades who died during the
war. This aspect of the poem, this positive note, is underscored by the
repetition of the opening verses at the end of the poem:

Qui pourra vous chanter si ce n'est votre frère d'armes, votre frère de sang
Vous Tirailleurs Sénégalais, mes frères noirs à la main chaude, couchés
sous la glace et la mort?

[Who but I should sing of you, your brother in arms, in blood
You, *tirailleurs* of Senegal, my black brothers, warm-handed sleeping under
ice and death.]

In view of this positive aspect of the poem, it would appear at the least
surprising that he would choose to dedicate the poem to Damas, whose
conception of the heroism of the Tirailleurs is radically different.

In the poem the first signs of social and political involvement also appear.
These themes were to dominate quite a few of the poems in this volume. In
spite of the poet's attachment to French culture, in fact one can speak of
love here, he finds it necessary to criticize France, not out of hatred but out
of love, like a mother pointing out with firmness, and if necessary chastise-
ment, the mistakes of her beloved child. Senghor puts it this way:

Je sais que ce peuple de feu, chaque fois qu'il a libéré ses mains
A écrit la fraternité sur la première page de ses monuments
Qu'il a distribué la faim de l'esprit comme de la liberté
A tous les peuples de la terre conviés solennellement au festin catholique.

[I know this fiery people, each time they have freed their hands,
Have written FRATERNITY on the first page of their monuments,
They have distributed hunger of the spirit and hunger of liberty
To all the peoples of the earth, solemnly called to the catholic feast.]

Is this a justification of his 'love' for France as opposed to Léon Damas' 'hatred' of the metropolis? He is basically accusing France here of hypocrisy, in politics as well as in philosophy. They are proclaimers of liberty but yet are out to enslave Africans. They cherish liberty yet are loath to grant it to others. They inspire in people a thirst for liberty, yet nourish them with nothing but intellectual and moral bankruptcy. He seems here to rejoin the Damas conception of life, except that he expresses himself with more tact, more discretion, with nuances, subtlety, enough to make his point but short of antagonizing the colonial masters. He plays the middle role, that of the conciliator, who seeks to bring the two sides together, replacing perhaps with understanding the love-hate dichotomy nurtured by discrimination and colonialism. His dedication of the poem to Damas is a call for understanding, for tolerance between the rulers and the ruled, the colonizers and the colonized, the whites and the blacks.

In *Hosties Noires* the poet enters into the racial and political scene. In the poem 'A l'Appel de la Race de Saba', dedicated to Pierre Achille, there is a new social involvement, a collective view of poetry, poetry in the service of revolution:

Nous étions là tous réunis, mes camarades les forts en thème et moi, tels aux premiers jours de guerre les nationaux débarqués de l'étranger
Et mes premiers camarades de jeu, et d'autres et d'autres encore . . .
Pour le dernier assaut contre les Conseils d'administration qui gouvernent les gouverneurs des colonies.

[There we were all together, my comrades those who were good at school and me, like countrymen who have just landed from abroad in the first days of a war
And my first playmates and others and still others . . .
For the last assault on the Administrative Councils that govern the governors of colonies.]

The poet and his friends are now attacking the sources of power, the administrative headquarters in Paris that send or issue instructions to the colonial representatives. He speaks at the same time about the bankers who have built their pink and white villas far from the industrial quarters, far from the native quarters filled with despair and misery. In this assault against the establishment he is no longer alone. It has taken on a universal dimension, like the internationalism of socialist workers. They were all there:

> Car nous sommes là tous réunis, divers de teint – il y en a qui sont couleur de café grillé, d'autres bananes d'or et d'autres terre des rizières
> Divers de traits de costume de coutumes de langue; mais au fond des yeux la même mélopée de souffrances à l'ombre des longs cils fiévreux
> Le Cafre le Kabyle le Somali le Maure, le Fân le Fôn le Bambara le Bobo le Mandiago
> Le nomade le mineur le prestataire, le paysan et l'artisan le boursier et le tirailleur
> Et tous les travailleurs blancs dans la lutte fraternelle.
> Voici le mineur des Asturies le docker de Liverpool le Juif chassé d'Allemagne, et Dupont et Dupuis et tous les gars de Saint-Denis.

> [For there we are all together, different colours ... some are the colour of roast coffee and others banana and golden, others like the earth in a ricefield
> Different features and dress customs and languages; but in the depths of the eyes the same chant of suffering beneath the long fevered lashes
> The Kaffir the Kabyle the Somali Moor, Fan Fon Bambara and Bobo and Mandiago
> Nomad and miner, moneylender, peasant and workman, student and soldier
> And all the white workers in the common struggle.
> See ... the miner of the Asturia the Liverpool docker the Jew driven out of Germany, Dupont, Dupuis and all the boys from Saint-Denis.]

The list is like a catalogue of the various groups of people and interests taking part in a demonstration. They are there to form a new kind of community, an international community to protect their collective interests in expectation of the dawn of a new transparent day.

Elsewhere, in the poem 'Méditerranée', the poet sings the memories of the memories of war, a kind of *metamemory*. In the heat of the war, in the evening as they get some respite from the sea-to-shore shelling, they speak about Africa, about their homes so far from Europe, so far away from the Mediterranean coast. If the memories of the continent far away were very refreshing during the war, the memories of these memories for Senghor were like revisiting old haunts, like a pilgrimage, not now to places of childhood fancy, but to the lands of exile.

C'était en Méditerranée, nombril des races claires, bleue comme jadis
océan n'ont vu mes yeux
Qui souriait de ses millions de lèvres de lumière . . .

Nous parlions de l'Afrique. . . .

Nous parlions du Fouta. . . .

Nous parlions du pays noir
Dans les cordages le soir, si près l'un de l'autre que nos épaules s'épousaient
fraternelles l'une à l'autre.
L'Afrique vivait là, au-delà de l'oeil profane du jour, sous son visage noir
étoilé. . . .

[It was in the Mediterranean, hub of the bright-skinned races, blue as no
ocean I have ever seen,
Smiling its million smiles of light . . .

We talked of Africa. . . .

We talked of Fouta. . . .

We talked of the black land
In the rigging, at evening so close to one another that our shoulders touched,
were brothers to one another.
Africa was alive there, beyond the day's profane eye, under his black starry
face . . .

Memories of those days fill Senghor with nostalgia just as happy memories of
childhood plunge him deep into an extended reverie. With his usual sharpness
of memory he can even recall the sound of the names of his favourite companion: "Et je redis ton nom: Dyallo! Et tu redis mon nom: Senghor!" The
name is mentioned to emphasize that those friends, those Senegalese fighters
were not just nonentities, black soldiers without names, without honour, but
men of flesh and blood, each one with his own individuality, his own destiny.
The acuity of the description – the star shining above, the last steps of the
tango, the woods around – confirm that it was a lived experience instead of a
merely romanticized one.

The poem coming after this in the collection seems to be a logical continuation. It is entitled 'Aux Tirailleurs Sénégalais Morts pour la France'. As if to
connect the thought dominating the poem 'Méditerranée' to this, he speaks of
'my dark brothers' whom no one cares to name, and who will die unremem-
bered. This same theme was also evident in the introductory poem. The poet
will not live to witness this anonymous treatment of comrades. He bids them
listen to him in their solitude under black earth and death, visionless, deprived

of the warmth and consolation of their companions as in the days when they lay down in the trenches. They were alone then, blanketed thrice with walls of darkness: the darkness of the skin, the grave and the night. There is another side to death in war – the memory of those who weep for the dead soldier. There are the women, the former wives who mourn for a few days, perhaps months before turning their hearts in other directions, to other pre-occupations. There are also the orphans implied by the thought of weeping mothers. Above all there are the friends who lived and fought with them, those comrades who also grew up with them. The memory of their death fills them with sadness because it also in some way presages their own death. The poet prays for the voice to hymn clearly the glory and honour of these friends, these comrades-in-arms. He addresses them as if they were still alive, and alive they still are in his memory:

> Ecoutez-nous, Morts étendus dans l'eau au profond des plaines du Nord et de l'Est
> Recevez ce sol rouge, sous le soleil d'été ce sol rougi du sang des blanches hosties
> Recevez le salut de vos camarades noirs, Tirailleurs sénégalais
>   MORTS POUR LA REPUBLIQUE!

> [Hear us, you dead, stretched out in the water deep in the plains of the North and the East
> Receive this red soil, beneath the summer sun this soil reddened with the blood of white hosts
> Receive the greetings of your black comrades, Senegalese *tirailleurs*
>   WHO HAVE DIED FOR THE REPUBLIC!]

They died for the French Republic, but they also died in the mind of the poet for the greater republic which is the world. They fought and died for the liberty of France, for the freedom of their own world, even though their own freedom as well as that of their wives, orphans and black comrades in Africa still had to be achieved. In days of evil and fear, during those days of sadness and forgetfulness, this was an eloquent testimony of friendship, of love, by one who had shared so much in common with those who fell in the battlefield. His praise of them is not that of 'ministers' but that of a friend and companion: 'Nous . . . vous apportons l'amitié de vos camarades d'âge.'

In the poem 'Luxembourg', it is the war and the approaching war which dominate the Luxembourg Gardens in Paris. The park is deserted except for two brave – or, rather, brash young boys playing tennis in the garden. It is autumn and the leaves are beginning to fall. Life seems on the wane, awaiting the winter of despair, the war. The signs are everywhere. There is the absence of children in the normally crowded Luxembourg Gardens. It is difficult to recognize the garden, now stripped of all memories, the footsteps of childhood, the memories of first love, sunny days passed by its pools, years fresh like the pool under the sun. These dreams of childhood have been swallowed up by the sad realities of life just as the dreams of his friends have been cut short by the sad realities of the battlefield. These comrades in the battlefield fall one by one, and in such numbers as the leaves from the trees in the Luxembourg Gardens. They blossom momentarily, grow old perhaps, fall because of age or wounds, are trampled underfoot. In the battlefield this is coupled with the flow of blood. In the garden soon the attendant arrives to collect the leaves. They are swept into a common container to be disposed of collectively, perhaps in an incinerator. In the battlefield, the dead are collected also for the sake of hygiene and put like the garden leaves in collective graves:

> Les voici qui tombent comme les feuilles avec les feuilles, vieillis blessés à
> mort piétinés, tout sanglants de sang.
> Que l'on ramasse pour quelle fosse commune?

> [See they fall like leaves among the leaves, old, wounded to death, trampled
> and stained with blood.
> Piled up for what common grave?]

Naturally it was difficult to see here the Luxembourg Gardens of better times. Soldiers on guard had replaced the frolicking children. Guns had been set up to protect the retreat of the Senators sitting in the Senate House within the garden premises. The chanting voices of carefree children would soon be replaced by the discordant sound of artillery shells and cries of pain and death. In other times, the trees and bushes around provided shelter, welcome to the young lovers embracing for the first time: a false kind of shelter, for there were a myriad eyes around – the eyes of nature if nothing else. There were other kinds of shelters now in the Luxembourg Gardens, trenches dug for the defending soldiers, pill-boxes erected for the ambushing soldiers. The autumn leaves continue to fall into the trenches. In those trenches also, like leaves, several soldiers will fall and die. For those dead, it would also have been a false and an insecure shelter. The blood of an entire generation will flow there like the fading leaves of an entire season. Perhaps also in spite of the sad tone of the poem, there is hope of spring, a rebirth after the winter of despair, death and disillusionment.

Hosties noires is a poetic vision of the Second World War. The poet himself took part in this war:

J'ai poussé en plein pays d'Afrique, au carrefour des castes des races et des
routes
Et je suis présentement soldat de deuxième classe parmi les humbles des
soldats.
                              (PRIÈRE DES TIRAILLEURS SÉNÉGALAIS)]

[I grew up deep in Africa, at the cross-roads of castes of races and routes
At present I am a private second class among ordinary soldiers.
                              (PRAYER FOR THE TIRAILLEURS OF SENEGAL)]

The central theme seems to be that of black victims who offer themselves, or
rather immolate themselves for the freedom and security of the world. It is
this very notion that is celebrated in the verses:

Tu le sais . . .
Et la plaine docile se fait jusqu'au non abrupt des volontaires libres
   Qui offraient leurs corps de dieux, gloire des stades, pour l'honneur
   catholique de l'homme.

[Thou knowest . . .
And the plain submits until the sharp 'no' of the free volunteers
   Who offered their godlike bodies, their athletic splendour, for the catholic
   honour of man.]

The poet loves the dramatic form and employs this quite regularly in his
poems. He now resorts to direct speech in order to express the deep emotion
he feels. The Senegalese soldiers now address their prayer to God. 'Sur cette
terre d'Europe débarqués, désarmés en armes laissés pour solde à la mort' is
the way their prayer begins. The poet in that single line expresses the situation
of the African arriving in France. He was probably also thinking of his own
disembarkation in 1928. They are disarmed, figuratively and physically. They
are in a new environment and do not quite know how to approach the situation.
For weapons they are not given the best but rather what has been rejected by
others. This echoes his earlier statement, that he is a private among this
group of ordinary soldiers: 'Je suis présentement soldat de deuxième classe
parmi les humbles des soldats.' It is a prayer of nostalgia, of regret, of sorrow:

Verrons-nous seulement mûrir les enfants nos cadets dont nous sommes les
   pères initiateurs? . .
Nous ne participerons plus à la joie sponsorale des moissons!
Nous n'entendons plus les enfants, oublieux du silence alentour et de
   pleurer les vivants
Les cris d'enfants parmi les sifflements joyeux des frondes et les ailes et la
   poussière d'or!
                              (PRIÈRE DES TIRAILLEURS SÉNÉGALAIS)

[Shall we ever see those children grow up, our younger brothers for whom
we stood initiatory fathers?
Take part again in the sponsorial joy of harvest?
We shall not hear the children any more, forgetting the silence that sur-
rounds us, forgetting to weep for the living
The shouts of children among the joyful rustling of leaves, among the gold
dust and the wings!

(PRAYER FOR THE TIRAILLEURS OF SFNEGAL)

It is a remembrance of things past, a revisiting from the dead of the world of
the living. The time for dancing is gone. From the world beyond, tears are
even memorable incidents, the harvest season is recalled with deep emotion.
Spring, summer, night, dawn, all assume special significance. The emphasis
is on loss, on the inability to participate again in the joys, sorrows, loves and
works of life: 'Oh! Toi qui sais si nous respirerons à la moisson, si de nouveau
nous danserons la danse de vie renaissante.' ['O Thou who knowest whether
we shall breathe at harvest, if we shall ever dance again the dance of renewing
life.'] The poem portrays the anxiety of the soldier before battle. It is a prayer
for courage, not courage to confront the battle ahead but courage to bear the
memories of things he might have to leave behind as a result of death. It is a
sweet and sour experience, the sweet savour of the past and a bitter anticipation
of the future. The soldier intones this supplication: 'Avant, oui avant l'odeur
future des blés et les vendanges dans l'ivresse, Que nous ne foulerons pas que
nous goûtions la douceur de la terre de France.' ['Before, yes before the future
smell of wheat and the wine harvest in its drunkenness, that we shall never
tread Let us taste the sweetness of the land of France']. There is also the
anxiety that the planter – here the soldier in the battlefield sowing the seeds
of victory and liberty – will live long enough to taste the harvest of joy and
freedom. The soldiers offer their bodies, together with those of their comrades
from France, to the Lord, even in death, for God also is the lord of armies, the
lord of the strong. Before the soldier stretches a mass of people, alike and
unlike but out there for the same purpose. 'Nous ne refusons pas l'intense
tension des minutes dernières, l'âpre douceur de la mort prochaine.' ['We
will not refuse the intense tension of the last minutes, the sharp sweetness of imminent death']. The poet remembers not only the last moments
before the attack but also the last weak seconds or seconds of weakness before
the assault. The poem ends with the dramatic words of the poet: 'Ecoute leurs
voix, Seigneur!' It is the poet who completes the prayer, who finishes the poem
for the soldier; the soldiers in question went to battle, and there as they
feared met their end, deprived of all. They were not there for the much-desired
harvest. They were not there for the final celebration of victory. They left

behind friends and family, wives and children, as they feared they would. It
is this thought that made the final seconds so bitter.

Senghor continues this eulogy of the Senegalese dead in his poem 'Camp
1940', dedicated to the *guelwar*, a warrior in Senegalese history. In ancient
times, the warrior in Africa had a name, some prestige. He could exhibit his
bravery and prowess, but this is not the case on the modern battlefield. In this
moving and eloquent elegy Senghor explains this:

Les plus purs d'entre nous sont morts: ils n'ont pu avaler le pain de honte.
Et nous voilà pris dans les rets,[1] livrés à la barbarie des civilisés
Exterminés comme des phacochères. Gloire aux tanks et gloire aux avions!

[The purest among us are dead. They could not swallow the bread of shame.
We are taken in the nets, delivered up to the barbarism of the civilized
Destroyed like warthogs. Glory be to tanks, glory be to aeroplanes!

TO THE GUELWAR]

War has lost its ancient glory. The knight, like the *guelwar*, can no longer
exhibit his individual strength. He can be annihilated without ever getting a
chance to fire a shot, to pull out his 'sword', superseded by tanks and recoilless
rifles, by aerial bombings and artillery fire. There is no glory in war. Modern
war is a kind of civilized barbarism. The truly valiant, the truly honest, the
truly pure rarely survive it. The most pure, says the poet, are unable to with-
stand the strain, not the strain of duty but rather that of boredom, that of
shame. The Senegalese soldiers are pictured as little birds that have fallen
from the cage and are unable to help themselves: 'Nous sommes des petits
d'oiseaux tombés du nid, des corps privés d'espoir et qui se fanent.' War has
become a big machine and individuals do not count any more. The world could
continue and does continue without them. It is perhaps this feeling that
evokes all the nostalgia in the poem '*Prière des Tirailleurs Sénégalais*'.
This nostalgia is accentuated by the discrimination in the French Army, in
France, this very country they had come to liberate, for which they were
going to shed their blood. Everywhere they looked for support, which was
not forthcoming. Perhaps that was why in their desolation they turned to
the Lord for solace:

Nous avons cherché un appui, qui croulait comme le sable des dunes
Des chefs, et ils étaient absents, des compagnons, ils ne nous reconnaissaient
    plus
Et nous ne reconnaissions plus la France.

[1] Prendre quelqu'un dans ses rets—to catch someone in one's toils.

It was difficult for them to recognize the France that invited them to help in its liberation. In the dead of night, they cried out their sorrow, they sounded their distress. Not a single voice responded or came to their rescue. The churches and their leaders were silent and quiet. The people and their leaders closed their eyes to their distress because they were black, as if being white was synonymous with humanity. Thoughts of the *guelwar* here bring some solace. The mere thought of the name is a source of honour, hope and resistance. They feel its inspiration. It inspires them with courage to fight, with hope that tomorrow will bring about equality and fraternity among the people of the world.

The concept of the immolation of the black man for the salvation of the world, especially the white world, crops up again in Senghor's poem 'Au Gouverneur Eboué'. There the poet speaks of thousands of people of diverse ethnic groups and tongues rising up at the inspiration of Governor Eboué, Governor General of French Equatorial Africa, rising up in arms for the defence of France, for the liberation of Europe:

Mille peuples et mille langues ont pris langue avec ta foi rouge
Voilà que le feu qui te consume embrase le désert et la brousse
Voilà que l'Afrique se dresse, la Noire et la Brune sa soeur.
L'Afrique s'est faite acier blanc, l'Afrique s'est faite hostie noire
Pour que vive l'espoir de l'homme.

[A thousand people and a thousand tongues have found voice in your red faith
See the fire that burns you inflames the desert and the bush
See Africa arises, the Black and the Brown her sister
Africa made white steel, Africa made black sacrifice
That the hope of Africa may live.]

This note of mild protest against the use of Senegalese soldiers for menial work is seen also in 'Camp 1940', dedicated to Abdoulaye Ly. In spite of the apparent insult, the soldiers refuse to desert, they do not revolt against their superiors in the army. If they accept these menial jobs, the poet explains, it is not because they are inferior racially but rather because of the nobility of their heart:

Ils ne partiront pas. Ils ne déserteront les corvées ni leur devoir de joie.
Qui fera les travaux de honte si ce n'est ceux qui sont nés nobles?

[They will not go. They will not leave their fatigues nor their duty of joy.
Who will do the lowest jobs if not those who were born noble?]

The poet remembers once again his comrades stretched out in the fields of

Europe, dead, along the highways of disaster. There the Senegalese prisoners lie prostrate along the roads of France. The perpetual laughter on their lips is gone. Gone is the black flower of African youth. These images dominate the poem 'Assassinats' in *Hosties noires*. The soldiers from Senegal were as it were assassinated on the streets of France, by machines and guns. The purity of those soldiers is alluded to in these verses:

> Et la forêt incoercible, victorieuse du feu et de la foudre.
> Le chant vaste de votre sang vaincra machines et canons
> Votre parole palpitante les sophismes et mensonges
> Aucune haine votre âme sans haine, aucune ruse votre âme sans ruse.

> [And the incoercible forest, victor over fire and thunder
> The immense song of your blood will conquer machines and mortars
> The pulse of your speech, lies and sophistry
> No hate your heart without hate, no guile your heart without guile.]

Their hearts and minds are pure, pure because they had nothing to do with the hatred in Europe, the hatred that brought about the war, the dead and the misery. In their village and country simplicity they were devoid of the sophistication characteristic of city life, of the glib insincerity that dominates human relations. As they lived, simple and innocent, so they also died not knowing what it was all about. It is for them that Senghor speaks: 'O Black martyrs immortal race, let me speak the words that forgive' – *O Martyrs noirs race immortelle, laissez-moi dire les paroles qui pardonnent*. Sometimes the innocence of these black martyrs assumes pathetic tones. Such is the case in the poem 'Taga de Mbaye Dyôb'. Senghor wants to sing his glory and honour. It is not because he killed several people, or fought bravely in war. He is praising him not because of his ancestry, for he perhaps has none worth remembering. It is not the type of honour filled with great achievements, brave deeds, daring exploits, giving up his life to save his friends. Nothing of the kind. It is 'a blank honour', for as the poet himself says, Mbaye Dyôb never so much as killed a rabbit:

> Dyôb! qui ne sais remonter ta généalogie et domestiquer le temps noir, dont
>   les ancêtres ne sont pas rythmés par la voix du tama
> Toi qui n'as tué un lapin, qui t'es terré sous les bombes des grands vautours
> Dyôb! – qui n'es ni capitaine ni aviateur ni cabalier pétaradant, pas seule-
>   ment du train des équipages
> Mais soldat de deuxième classe au Quatrième Régiment des Tirailleurs
>   sénégalais
> Dyôb! – je veux chanter ton honneur blanc.

[Dyob! You cannot trace back your ancestry and bring order into black history, your forefathers are not sung by the voice of the tama.
You who have never killed a rabbit, who went to ground under the bombs of the great vultures,
Dyob! you who are not captain or airman or trooper, not even in the baggage train,
But a second-class private in the Fourth Regiment of the Senegal Rifles
Dyob, I will celebrate your white honour.]

To emphasize the role of the Senegalese soldier, the poet has chosen the least known among them. By naming him he confers on him some personality. The poetic monument he is erecting for him is not just for an unknown soldier, but for a particular soldier, the least known perhaps. The young girls will erect triumphal arches in his honour and together they will sing his praises, how he braved more than death, more than the tanks, the planes beyond the power of sorcery. They will sing of how he braved famine, cold and humiliation as a captive soldier, how he refused to desert his companions so as not to break the silent contract, knowing that a soldier less means more work for those remaining, aware that a face less means mourning for those left behind, and that a smile less means greater sorrow for all concerned. From coast to coast, young virgins will sing in his honour, in praise of Dyôb: 'Dyôb! – je dis ton nom et ton honneur.' Returning to a purely personal note, the poet gives us another view of camp life during the war. In his 'Lettre à un prisonnier', the poet, himself a prisoner, writes to another:

Je t'écris dans la solitude de ma résidence surveillée – et chère – de ma peau noire.
Heureux amis, qui ignorez les murs de glace et les appartements trop clairs qui stérilisent
Toute graine sur les masques d'ancêtres et les souvenirs mêmes de l'amour.

[I write to you from the solitude of my residence which is under watch. The dear residence of my black skin.
Lucky friends, who have never known walls of ice and rooms so bright they sterilize
Every seed on the masks of the ancestors, and even the memories of love.]

One of the most moving poems in this series is the poem 'Aux Soldats Négro-Américains', dedicated to Mercer Cook. Senghor goes beyond Senegal now and finds new inspiration at the sight of black American soldiers. They too were innocent like the soldiers from Senegal. They had come to liberate France. Their hands were clean. They were discriminated against. They thus

had much in common with the Senegalese, except that they were well
equipped and used to the machines of destruction. They were so much a part
of the violence of western man that the African poet could hardly recognize
them as they drove their weapons of destruction to kill and knock down
churches, cathedrals and homes. Covered with their helmets they were
difficult to recognize, but only a touch of their hands and the poet recognized,
or rather felt in them the sons of Africa, the sons of ancient Africa. They still
had the warmth of their tropical homeland, those smiles of peasant simplicity,
those ancient voices rumbling like the cascades of the Congo. Whereas
most of the Senegalese soldiers fell without firing a shot, the black Americans
bombed cathedrals and cities:

> Frères, je ne sais si c'est vous qui avez bombardé les cathédrales, orgueil de
>   l'Europe
> Si vous êtes la foudre dont la main de Dieu a brûlé Sodome et Gomorrhe.
> Non, vous êtes les messagers de sa merci, le souffle du Printemps après
>   l'Hiver. . . .
> Vous apportez le printemps de la Paix et l'espoir au bout de l'attente. . . .
>
> Vous leur apportez le soleil.

> [Brothers, I do not know if it was you who bombed the cathedrals, the pride
>   of Europe
> If you are the lightning that in God's hand burnt Sodom and Gomorrah.
> No, you are the messengers of his mercy, breath of Spring after Winter.
> For those who had forgotten laughter (using only an oblique smile)
> Who had forgotten the salt taste of tears and the irritant smell of blood
> You bring the springtime of Peace, hope at the end of waiting. . . .
>
> You bring the sun.]

Finally he addresses them as black brothers, as messengers of peace: 'Frères
noirs, guerriers dont la bouche est fleur qui chante . . . Oh! délice de vivre
après l'Hiver . . . je vous salue comme des messagers de paix.' ['Black brothers,
warriors whose mouths are singing flowers . . . O delight to live after Winter
. . . I greet you as the messengers of peace.'] But thinking of the Senegalese
soldiers, for reasons of emotion and nationality closer to him, he has some
difficulty in viewing them with the same eye of optimism as he does the
Americans. In 'Tyaroye' nostalgia overtakes him again as he thinks of black
prisoners, francophone prisoners. The thought becomes more painful when
he thinks of France forgetting the blood of those that saved her, of treating as
second-class French citizens those who fought for her liberation. Rhetorically
he asks:

Et votre sang n'a-t-il pas ablué la nation oublieuse de sa mission d'hier?
Dites, votre sang ne s'est-il mêlé au sang lustral de ses martyrs?

[And has not your blood washed the nation that now forgets the mission she
once had?
Tell me, has not your blood mingled with the lustral blood of her martyrs?]

Certainly they did not die in vain, he affirms. It was real blood they shed and
not lukewarm water. With strength and courage it nurtures Africa's hope of a
better future, a hope that will be realized at twilight:

Non, vous n'êtes pas morts gratuits. Vous êtes les témoins de l'Afrique
immortelle
Vous êtes les témoins du monde nouveau qui sera demain.

Dormez ô Morts! et que ma voix vous berce, ma voix de courroux que
berce l'espoir.

[No you did not die for nothing you who are dead! This blood is not
lukewarm water.
Thickly it waters our hope which will blossom at twilight.
It is our thirst, our hunger for honour, those great absolute princes
No, you did not die for nothing. You are witnesses of undying Africa
You are witnesses of the new world that will be tomorrow.

Sleep O Dead, and let my voice cradle you, my voice of anger cradled by
hope.]

The final verse could be considered the final words of the entire volume, even
though there is another poem that follows, in fact the longest in the series. It is
like the last prayer said by the minister as he leaves the cemetery where dead
soldiers are buried. 'Sleep O Dead! and let my voice cradle you, my voice of
anger cradled by hope.' It is a wish for all the dead. There, in that last line,
meet the sorrows of the past and the hopes of future, the sufferings gone and
the aspirations to come. Hatred gradually turning to love, despair gradually
giving rise to hope. Death announcing, in a way, new life. The old world dies
with the dead who sacrificed their lives to redeem it. A new world is born with
the new hope they have inspired.

The poem was written in December 1944, perhaps around Christmas, for it
carried a message of forgiveness, message of hope, message of love, message
of – above all – peace. This naturally leads to the final poem of the volume
entitled 'Prière de paix', dedicated to Georges and Claude Pompidou. If
'Tyaroye' is the final prayer at the graveyard, 'Prière de paix' is the requiem
mass at the church. It opens with great sounds of a deep organ and the Latin

phrase echoing behind' . . . *sicut et nos dimitimus debitoribus nostris'* – as we forgive those that trespass against us – here it is the temptation of anger, hatred, the desire for revenge. The prayer for peace is a fight against all these evils. '*Et ne nos inducas in tentationem, sed libera nos a malo.*' [And lead us not into temptation, but deliver us from evil.]

From here on the poet prays for everyone, above all for Africa, for the exploited black man:

> Seigneur pardonne à ceux qui ont fait des Askia des maquisards, de mes princes des adjudants
> De mes domestiques des boys et de mes paysans des salariés, de mon peuple un peuple prolétaires. . . .
> Car il faut bien que Tu oublies ceux qui ont exporté dix millions de mes fils dans les maladreries de leurs navires
> Qui en ont supprimé deux cents millions.

> [Lord, forgive them who turned the Askia into maquisards, my princes into sergeant-majors
> My household servants into 'boys', my peasants into wage-earners, my people into a working class. . . .
> For Thou must forget those who exported ten millions of my sons in the leper-houses of their ships
> Who killed two hundred millions of them.]

The serpent of hatred appears but is suppressed in the heart of the poet, who nevertheless continues to denounce slavery, colonialism, France that hates occupation but does not hesitate to occupy Africa; France that receives French soldiers with pomp and festivity but treats the Senegalese soldiers as mercenaries; France that claims it is a Republic and yet would divide up Africa and allot parcels as concessions to individuals and businesses. The poet wants nothing to do with this kind of France, untrue to itself. He prefers instead to remember the France that gave him his faith, his education:

> Bénis ce peuple qui m'a apporté Ta Bonne Nouvelle, Seigneur, et ouvert mes paupières lourdes à la lumière de la foi.
> Il a ouvert mon coeur à la connaissance du monde, me montrant l'arc-en-ciel des visages neufs de mes frères

> [Bless this people who brought me Thy Good News, Lord, and opened my heavy eyelids to the light of faith.
> Who opened my heart to the understanding of the world, showing me the rainbow of fresh faces that are my brothers.]

In prayer for unity, hope, faith and peace, the poet wishes and prays for a union of all hands in a fraternal way below God's given peace as soldiers and people march below the triumphal arcs, rainbow-shaped, not only to signify that there should be no more wars, but to indicate that people of all colours and ideas should live fraternally together, like the colours of the rainbow.

Éthiopiques

Éthiopiques

▼▼▼▼▼▼▼▼▼▼▼▼▼▼▼▼▼▼▼▼▼▼▼▼▼▼▼▼▼▼▼▼▼▼▼

Hosties noires is easily the most homogeneous volume of Senghor's poetry, from the point of view not only of theme but also of language and sentiment. But in *Éthiopiques* there is diversity of theme, sentiment, language, emotion. The preparation of the volume was announced around 1948, but it was only published in 1956, mostly because of the intense involvement of the poet in political activities, events that are more than merely reflected in the volume. The poet seems to have attained full poetic maturity. His poetry becomes guided by certain basic principles which he would articulate himself in the 'post-face' to the volume, which he calls: 'Comme les lamantins vont boire à la source' ['How the sea-cows will drink from the spring'].

One of the more striking poems in this collection is 'Congo', where Senghor celebrates the properties of the great black African river. One might wonder why he chose the Congo River rather than the River Niger, which stretches across West Africa. It is probably because of the sound of the name, the full-mouthed sounds of the vowel 'o', which seems to underscore its greatness and the richness of its resources and properties:

> Oho! Congo oho! Pour rythmer ton nom grand sur les eaux sur les fleuves
> sur toute mémoire
> Que j'émeuve la voix des kôras Koyaté! . . .

> [Oho! Congo oho! I move the voices of the *koras* of Koyaté to make your
> great name their rhythm
> Over the waters and rivers, over all I remember . . .]

The river in most societies is considered a source of life, of new life in particular: a source of ablution and purification. In the poem, Senghor looks at the Congo River as lying in a bed of forest, 'reine sur l'Afrique domptée, que les phallus des monts portent haut ton pavillon'. The river is also considered the source of life, like a woman that generates life. The river is the mother of everything that has nostrils, all that can breathe, in short of all that lives, including creatures as dangerous as the crocodile, and as big as the hippopotamus, sea-cows, iguanas, fishes, birds. The river is the source of human life also, for thanks to its tides and floods, the fields that feed man are themselves nourished. She is an immense woman. In her bosom swim canoes as the paddles stroke along the sides.

There is a total personification of the river. This is not very far removed from the anthropomorphism and pantheism that characterize certain elements in African traditional religion. What strikes one here is the diversity of properties associated with the River Congo. Addressing the river directly, the poet says:

Ma Saô mon amante aux cuisses furieuses, aux longs bras de nénuphars calmes

[My Sao my lover with maddened thighs, with long calm waterlily arms]

The poet therefore refers at the same time to the striking waves of the river and also the long stretch of lilies that grace the river banks, cool and calm on a mild afternoon.

This attribution of a feminine nature to the Congo becomes more evident when the poet starts describing its properties and qualities by adopting the surrealist method of endless enumeration.

Femme précieuse d'ouzougou, corps d'huile imputrescible à la peau de nuit diamantine.

[Precious woman of *ouzougou* body of imputrescible oil, skin of diamantine night.]

One thinks immediately of an earlier poem by Senghor, 'Femme noire', where the same surrealist technique is also used effectively. The river thus becomes a creature of flesh and blood, that feels sentiments of joy and sorrow, beautiful and attractive like any young woman of outstanding qualities and temperament. All around, the mountains sing the praises and proclaim the greatness of the river. They also serve to defend the woman-river and protect her against unwarranted intrusions. Hence the line: 'Que les phallus des monts portent haut ton pavillon'. What is referred to here is the standard ('pavillon') of victory, the flag of triumph, the colours of independence and self-sufficiency. The qualities that come up again and again are those of gems, precious stones, 'corps d'huile imputrescible' expertly oiled, lubricated to continue the flow of life and avoid the clash of the creatures within its bosom. 'A la peau de nuit diamantine' signifies not only the beauty of this river, black and African, but its greatness, durability, preciousness, like the gem diamond. And of course not far away are the diamond mines of Katanga. The river, then, is considered the source of these natural resources, the mother of these objects lodged in her bed and bosom.

The poet then sings the beauties and attributes of the goddess that is the River Congo:

> Toi calme Déesse au sourire étale sur l'élan vertigineux de ton sang
> O toi l'impaludée de ton lignage, délivre-moi de la surrection de mon sang.
> Tamtam toi toi tamtam des bonds de la panthère, de la stratégie des fourmis
> Des haines visqueuses au jour troisième surgies du potopoto des marais.

> [Calm Goddess with your smile that rides the dizzy surges of your blood
> Malarious by your descent, deliver me from the surrection of my blood.
> Drum drum you drum, from the panther's spring, the ant's strategy
> From the viscous hates risen on the third day from the mud of the marshes.]

The Congo River is the calm goddess, it is the tomtom that sends ripples of messages across the country, the continent: the tomtom, with undulating movements like the jumps of the panther, meandering through the forest like a swarm of locusts. The river is a protector and a guide. It guides the wanderer, the traveller, the explorer through the forests. It is a source of comfort in the dark night, a reassuring creature in the mysterious silence of the forests. It keeps a watchful vigil for the forests.

The poet's conception of the river here is very much like his image of the black woman. The treatment is of the same kind and the vocabulary he uses has similarities. Thus when the poet says:

> Mon amante à mon flanc, dont l'huile fait docile mes mains mon âme
> Ma force s'érige dans l'abandon, mon honneur dans la soumission

> [My lover at my side, whose oil makes docile my hands my heart
> My strength is set up in abandon, my honour in submission]

one thinks of the black woman to whom the same words and description could be applied. The emphasis here is on the captivating force of the river, like that of the woman. The sight of the splendour of the river is enough to warm even an obdurate heart. The force of the river, very much like that of a woman, lies in its *abandonment*, its total sacrifice of self. Like every other thing African, in the Senghorian system of values it is rhythm that dominates the life of the Congo. The poet draws his knowledge from instinctive union with the rhythm of the Congo River. In a very alliterative line, the poet seems to underscore the rhythm he has been celebrating:

> Rythmez clochettes rythmez langues rythmez rames la danse du Maître des rames.

> [Ring out bells, sing out tongues, beat out oars the dance of the Master of oars]

The bells that toll symbolize the Christianity that has planted itself along the banks of the River Congo. Side by side with the sound of bells are the sounds of the tomtom signifying a symbiosis, a continuation of the old and the traditional. The bells have their own charm and rhyme and rhythm too. Diverse as is the concatenation of the church bells, there is also a diversity of languages, of tongues as the Congo River meanders from one ethnic group to another, unifying the groups and absorbing the rhythm in each language into its waves and movements. All along the navigable parts of the river, there is also the rhythm of the paddles, as fishermen go to the goddess for fish, their source of livelihood; as farmers cross the river to sell their products; as a young couple in early evening takes a ride across the river to see some distant relations. Naturally these memories remind the poet of his childhood in Senegal, and of the rivers there. He too used to cross the river Senegal to pay a visit to his relations in English-speaking Gambia. He saw these fishermen on the river, and felt and heard the variety of rhythms he now transposes to the River Congo. He too lived in Paris and saw the movement of the River Seine as it flowed under its many bridges, with the boats floating along. It had its own rhythm, its own charm, its own femininity. The English poet Spenser, writing about the River Thames, said: 'Sweet Thames run softly till I end my song.' The French poet Apollinaire also sang of the River Seine: 'Sous le pont Mirabeau coule la Seine et nos amours.' Langston Hughes sings of rivers too. In his poem 'The Negro Speaks of Rivers', he writes:

I've known rivers ancient as the world and older than the flow of human
  veins
My soul has grown deep like the rivers
I have bathed in the Euphrates when dawns were young,
I built my hut near the Congo and it lulled me to sleep,
I looked upon the Nile and raised the pyramids above it.

And Walt Whitman sings of rivers in his poem 'Crossing Brooklyn Ferry':

Flood-tide below me! I see you face to face! . . .

The impalpable sustenance of me from all things at hours of the day. . . .

The current rushing so swiftly and swimming with me far away,
The others that are to follow me, the ties between me and them. . . .

Flow on, river! flow with the flood-tide, and ebb with the ebb-tide!
Frolic on, crested and scallop-edg'd waves!
Gorgeous clouds of the sunset! drench with your splendour me, or the men
  and women generations after me!

Quite understandably, rivers, lakes and oceans have fascinated poets for generations. But here again, as in his other poems, Senghor adds a novel dimension to the admiration of rivers. It is no longer the River Seine, or the Brooklyn River, but a black and African river that he praises, just as he sang the beauty of the black woman. The scenery is African. We see the canoe, and the triumphant choirs of Fadiouth (in Senegal) are evoked. We hear the sound of the tomtom, the clapping of hands, the chants of forty virgins, glittering arrows, cowris, and lilies around the tropical waters, and high above them the traditional bamboos of African water-fronts. The poem itself is written to be accompanied with music, three koras and a balafong. It is for this reason that at the beginning of the poem Senghor emphasizes the ineffectiveness of words in the description of the Congo River. It is something that has to be felt. It is the rhythm of life itself. It defies description. The local colour is of course seen in the type of animals that people the waters of the Congo: iguanas, crocodiles, hippopotami, and the ever-present *lamantins* (sea-cows). The beauty of darkness hangs over the river from the beginning to the end.

Le Kaya-Magan marks an accentuation of the colours of darkness. The domain is that of darkness and night:

Kaya-Magan je suis! la personne première
Roi de la nuit noire de la nuit d'argent, Roi de la nuit de verre.

[Kaya-Magan am I! the first person
King of the black night of the white night and of the night of silver King of the night of glass.]

As with the Congo River, among all the creatures that inhabit the river, that surround its banks, that make use of its resources; here again in the great dark river that is night, in the great dark space or void that is the domain of darkness, there are also kings and queens, the strong and the weak. In short there is also a hierarchy of values, of strengths and weaknesses. The Kaya-Magan is the king of the dark night, the glittering silvery night – a clear reference to the stars; the king of the transparent night – a reference both to the transparency of the moonlit night and to the reflection of the moon on the waters of the countryside. In this Senghorian sky, there are more than twelve thousand stars lit up like candles in the heavens.

Politically, philosophically, Senghor has been a middle-of-the-roader, a man of conciliation and mediation. This theme of union was in a way in vogue with the surrealist leaders, who also sought to find the point of junction between the living and the dead, the spiritual and the material, the religious and the lay. Here Kaya-Magan is presented as the king that unites the night and the day, the north and the south, the east and the west. The political

dimensions of the symbols are evident. Night and day not only represent two
contraries, but in the solar hierarchy of races could well represent the dark and
the coloured races. His wish is also that of harmony between the princes of the
North, Europe, and the rulers of the South, Africa. When he speaks of the
rising sun and the setting sun, in short the east and the west, one thinks of the
increasing rift at the period of his writing between the western world and
eastern world, between the capitalist system and the communist and socialist
systems. It is in this light that Kaya-Magan presents himself as the conciliator:

> Je dis KAYA-MAGAN je suĩ̃   ̃i de la lune, j'unis la nuit et le jour
> Je suis Prince du Nord du Sud, du Soleil-levant Prince et du Soleil-
>   couchant
> La plaine ouverte à mille ruts, la matrice où se fondent les métaux
>   précieux . . .

> [I say Kaya-Magan am I! King of the moon, I join the night and the day
> I am prince of the North of the South, of Sunrise prince and of Sunset
> A plain lying open to a thousand lusts, the womb and foundry of precious
>   metals . . .]

It is significant to note the preponderance of feminine qualities and images in
this poem, as in other poems of Senghor. He not only speaks of 'la douceur
féminine de la nuit'; he adds:

> Mon empire est celui des proscrits de César, des grands bannis de la raison
>   ou de l'instinct
> Mon empire est celui d'Amour, et j'ai faiblesse pour toi femme

> [My empire is over those banished by Caesar, the great outlaws of reason
>   and instinct
> My empire is the empire of Love, and my weakness is for you woman]

Night is the time of dreams, the time for romance, reverie, wanderings and
imagination. All this is symbolized by 'Kaya-Magan', 'le mouvement du
tamtam, force de l'Afrique future'. Here again we find the Senghorian
conception that Africans and blacks in general are endowed with feminine
qualities: artistic, musical and creative. The future strength of Africa, he
intimates, lies in the sound of the tomtom, the disarming rhythm of life. By
implication, it is not materialism, science, engineering or economics that will
save the continent but rather the spiritual force, the mystic force of the people,
of nature itself. Hence, Kaya-Magan is not the Prince of gold, or ivory. He is
not the lord of the world, the material world, but lord of the mystic world,
lord of the stars, the moon; he is the god who rules night and day. Kaya-
Magan might himself generate gold (*le roi de l'or – qui a la splendeur du midi*,

la douceur féminine de la nuit) but he is not attached to it because his veritable empire is that of Love, that empire where the wise, the rational, the logical are banished (*Mon empire est celui des proscrits de César, des grands bannis de la raison ou de l'instinct*). Where else can one find this irrational, illogical world (not in the pejorative sense, but merely denoting the absence of, or lack of reason or logic) but in the realm of dreams, the moon, the night, darkness, in a kind of surrealistic world where these positive appendages of modern science and technology are looked down upon or ignored? There is a difference between the surrealist norm and the Senghorian philosophy. The difference is basically one of degree. For the surrealists, their effort, and an effort only, was to discover the point where reality and dream merge into one. For Senghor, for Kaya-Magan, this principle is already possessed, already a part of the ancestral culture.

One remarkable aspect of *Éthiopiques* is the symbolism of flora and fauna and their significance within the general philosophy and works of Senghor. The poem that opens *Éthiopiques* is entitled 'L'Homme et la Bête'. In the entire poem, there is a fascinating enmeshing of man and beast in a web of symbols, in a pantheistic kind of world. Again the time is of great importance here. *Éthiopiques* is the dark kingdom of Africa. It is evening in the poem in question: 'Je te nomme Soir ô Soir ambigu'. It is naturally the dreamlike quality of night that confers on it this ambiguous nature. It is a time of darkness but also one of clairvoyance. It is the time of total silence, yet life is active. It is primarily to demonstrate this ambiguity that Senghor adds:

C'est l'heure des peurs primaires, surgies des entrailles d'ancêtres.

[It is the hour of primal terrors; they rise from the bowels of the ancestors.]

The 'Peurs primaires' the poet is talking about are very familiar to the child brought up in the village where night is dark and eerie and lacks the destructive brilliance of modern neon lights. Senghor as a child lived in such a village, Joal. It is doubly interesting to remark that in *Éthiopiques*, in the 'post-face', the poet draws the reader's attention to this aspect of his life:

And since I must explain myself with respect to my own poems, I will confess again that almost all the beings and things evoked in them come from my region: a few Serere villages lost in the tide-covered lands, the woods, creeks and the fields. Their name alone is enough to make me relive the kingdom of childhood – and the reader with me, I hope – 'through a forest of symbols'. I have lived once with the shepherds and the farmers . . . I have therefore lived in this kingdom, seen with my eyes, and heard with my ears the fabulous beings beyond the sensible world: . . . the crocodiles, guardians of the fountains, the sea-cows, that used to sing in the stream, the dead of the village and the ancestors, who used to speak to me, initiating me into the alternating verities of darkness and noon.

It is in this perspective that poems in *Éthiopiques*, especially those composed expressly for this volume, should be read. In particular, the opening poem 'L'Homme et la Bête' should be read with this in mind. The two words 'peurs primaires' viewed in isolation are not perhaps sufficiently meaningful. But read in the light of Senghor's life and philosophy, they are full of meaning and symbolism. The two words evoke right away all the precious fears, nightmares, and shocks of childhood: precious in that the adult who has long ago lost his innocence would want to, but cannot, relive them. Of course they are precious only in retrospect, for the child in the moment of fear and nightmare has no perspective. The inaccessibility of objects makes them more precious: hence 'precious fears'.

In 'L'Homme et la Bête', these precious fears are seen again by the adult, not as obstacles to be removed but as induplicable elements of nature to be preserved. In the domain of ambiguous night, there is everything. The silence and inactivity of the night has already been mentioned. But the night in a way is more active and more populated than the day, because then the dead rise again according to traditional lore and patrol and relive their existences. The world population at night is thus more than doubled. There are also the animals that fear to move around during the day. At night they roam freely, not to ravage but to live out their lives unmolested by man and nature. There is

la Bête dans la boue féconde qui nourrit tsétsés stégomyas
Crapauds et trigonocéphales, araignées à poison caïmans à poignards.

[But the Beast is without form in the fecund mud, breeding mosquito and tsetse
Toads and wedge-headed serpents, poisonous spiders, caymans with mouths of cactus.]

In the night, 'Un long cri de comète traverse la nuit, une large clameur rythmée d'une voix juste' – ['A long cry crosses the night like a comet, a great clamour made rhythmic by a pitched voice.'] The voice is not that of a comet but that of an animal. Man is joyous as he destroys other creatures in uneven combat, but there is in the distance the frightening roar of the lion, whose eyes alone are enough to kill. The lion, as in all literature, is here considered lord of the animal world, 'seigneur des forces imbéciles'. After this discordant note of fear, the poet ends the poem with tranquillity:

Le lac fleurit de nénuphars, aurore du rire divin.

[The lake blooms with lilies, dawn of the divine laughter.]

The creatures of the night depart. The toads and the frogs silence their voices that have disturbed the ponds all night. The tsetse flies also retire at the approaching light of day. The lion withdraws from human eyes. The spider lies quiet in its nest. Man awakes in the morning and sees nothing but the lilies flowering on the lake, like a transcendental smile from the god of dawn, initiating the spectator after a night of dreams and hallucinations into the verities of the noon and the day, or in the words of Senghor, 'aux vérités alternée de la nuit et du midi'.

In 'Teddungal', Senghor continues this picture of man and beast living side by side, as in the villages of Africa. There is the human procession along the lake that cooled and soothed their feet. An easterly wind fills eyes and nostrils; the throat is filled with emotions emanating from the heart. The picture here is that of a young man on his way to meet the bride and the loved one. But along the roads also, as in fairy tales, there are other creatures that deserve attention because of their manners and their dress: there is the scorpion, and also the cameleon, the apes, and other creatures.

Or les scorpions furent de sable, les camélions de toutes couleurs. Or les rires des singes secouaient l'arbre des palabres, comme peau de panthère les embûches zébraient la nuit.
Mille embûches des puissants: chaque touffe d'herbes cache un ennemi.

[And the scorpions were of sand, the chameleons of every colour. And the laughter of monkeys shook the palaver tree; like panther skin, ambushes striped the night.
The thousand ambushes of the mighty: every tuft of grass hides an enemy.]

In keeping with the theme of *Éthiopiques*, the journey takes place at night, just as dew is beginning to fall over tropical leaves, just as the cock is about to crow for the first time and just before the dogs start to bark at the receding moon.

Important also in the Senghorian vision is the symbolism of trees. The night is referred to as the 'feuille mobile'. The baobab tree, which is very common in Senegal, is present everywhere. In 'L'Homme et la Bête' Senghor writes that

Les kaïcédrats sont émus dans leurs racines douloureuses.

[The kaicedrats are moved to their dolorous roots.]

There are the lakes where the lilies flower. The Congo, as seen already, is like a woman 'aux cuisses furieuses, aux longs bras de nénuphars calmes'. In 'Messages' one reads also of the clouds that presage 'verdant fields', and of the acacias, symbol of the dry season. In 'L'Absente' the maidens have necks of roses. But it is the poem 'Congo' that reunites man, beast and the trees. For the river is the queen of all and nourishes all without exception, without favoritism:

> Noue son élan
> le coryphée
> A la proue de son sexe, comme le fier chasseur de lamantins.
> Rythmez clochettes rythmez langues rythmez rames la danse du Maître des rames.

> [The leader
> of the dance makes fast his vigour
> To the prow of his sex, like the proud hunter of the manatees.
> Ring out bells, sing out tongues, beat out oars the dance of the Master of oars.]

He begins the poem 'Messages' very much in the same manner. There are two points to be noted here. He writes:

> Il m'a dépêché un cheval du Fleuve sous l'arbre des palabres mauve.

Here we have the local colour of horses and rivers. Instead of saying that a messenger came, he describes what brought him, signifying that more important than the bearer of the message is the bearer of the bearer. It is also the local idiomatic expression. For in some villages today, where horses are rare and cars are rarer still, when announcing the arrival of a man by one or the other means, the villagers merely say that 'a car came' or that 'a horse came'. This must not be taken to indicate a dehumanization of the individual. Rather by mechanizing himself the individual has already caused his dehumanization, and the villager is merely reflecting what he sees before him – a big animal or a monstrous machine rolling up dust behind it, polluting the air of the tropical sky and rumbling along the unpaved road, disturbing the peace and frightening children and adults alike. There is, nevertheless, a great difference between the horse and the car. Horses, livery and stable are signs of affluence. Horses have grace, the machine has none. With Senghor, therefore, if the lion is the king of beasts, the horse is the servant of the king or the noble. In 'Messages', the poet writes:

Cinquante chevaux seront ton escorte, tapis de haute laine et mille pas
Et des jeunes gens à livrée d'espoir. Il te précède vêtu de sa pourpre
Qui te vêt et son haut bonnet t'éclaire, son épée nue t'ouvre la voie des
   enthousiasmes. . . .

[Fifty horses will be your escort, carpet of thick pile and a thousand paces
And young men in the livery of hope. He goes before you clad in purple
Which clothes you also and his high bonnet lights your way, his naked
sword opens up for you the way of enthusiasm.]

This is understandable, in Senegal in particular, where wealth used to be
measured by the number of horses or head of cattle the particular family
possessed, and where dowry was sometimes paid in cattle. But in Senghor's
poetry, horses are not just the object of commerce and the instrument of
voyages, they seem to have a personality, they are respected, adorned. In
'Teddungal', already referred to, movement is also described with the beast of
burden as the point of reference:

Nous marchions par le Dyêri au pas du boeuf-porteur – l'aile du cheval
   bleu est pour les Maîtres-de-Saint-Louis – mais nos pieds dans la
   poussière des morts et nos têtes parées de nulle poudre d'or.

[We walked across the Dyeri at the pace of a laden ox – the wing of the blue
   horse is for the Masters-of-Saint-Louis – but our feet in the dust of the
   dead and our heads unadorned with powdered gold.]

In the poem 'L'Absente', good news is announced across the hills, along the
pathways by 'les chameliers au long cours' ['the far-travelling camel-drivers'].
The centre of attraction again is the carrier of the bearer of the news. This is
very easy to explain. As the poet himself said in the seventh stanza of
'L'Absente':

Car à quoi bon le manche sans la lame et la fleur sans le fruit?

[For what good is the handle without the blade and the flower without the
   fruit?]

In short, the horse and the messenger are inseparable: one is a fulfilment of
the other and one is useless without the other. Therefore, it is a life of mutual
need and co-operation, and not one of antagonism and competition.

One of the most interesting poems in *Éthiopiques* is 'A New York'. New
York has always fascinated foreign poets, among whom one should mention
Federico García Lorca of Spain, who spent some time there between 1929 and
1930 and wrote poems about Harlem, the black quarter within the metro-

politan city of New York, and criticized the massive structure and dehumanization of beings in Manhattan. There is also the Russian poet Yevgeny Yevtushenko, who after a journey to the United States of America and a visit to New York wrote about his impressions of this city that has both fascinated and ruined many:

> Someone is lying about stability
> While there is slush in New York
> Someone is telling a fairy tale of a firm road
> Although the road is slippery.

Lorca, who in his poetry and more so in his drama is always leading a fight for the poor, the cheated, the neglected, here in Harlem is out to denounce all the people that ignore and neglect one half of the city: the blacks, the poor, the immigrants, the unredeemed half of society, the unenfranchised. He denounces the rigid structures of the offices that seem not only to keep the unfortunate half out of jobs but also keep the privileged from seeing the misery of the unfortunate. When Yevtushenko in his 'Slush in New York' talks about the slippery nature of the city, he is talking about the slippery nature of life. He has in mind not physical stability but rather stability for the soul, psychological stability, emotional balance, social harmony, racial understanding, economic justice. For him, from the outside, there is a feeling of stability viewed as it were from the massive structures that are the skyscrapers of New York. There is for the onlooker a vision of stability and emotional balance on the faces of the New Yorkers that stroll along the United Nations Plaza, that hustle along Fifth Avenue; that gaze with steadiness on the counters of Wall Street; that smile in the offices along Madison Avenue. There is a feeling of stability, but behind the structures, behind the smiles, inside the minds of the players, life is slippery, life is slipping because of drugs, ambition, lack of peace of mind. In short, 'no one' is telling a fairy tale of a firm road. Rather it is the poet that sees what others believe, and he knows as they do that the massive structure in front hides an emptiness behind.

Senghor talks about the same feelings, the same inequities, the 'dryness' in the hearts of New Yorkers. But there are other dimensions to his poem that make it perhaps more exciting, more controversial and richer than the other poems about New York.

For Senghor, the disappointment was total on his arrival in New York as a member of the French delegation to the United Nations. He speaks about confusing the outside beauty of New York with the reality of life itself, and by extension confusing real life with the physical beauty of the long-legged maidens in nylon stockings. He talks about his timidity, awe, respect in front of the massive structures, the sky-scrapers of New York, a sight that never fails to astonish the foreigner arriving in the United States. Leaving the airport, he sees the massive cars, the gyrating roads, underpasses, over-passes, fly-overs, crossroads, forked roads, bridges, tunnels as he moves at fearsome speed or crawls at an exasperatingly slow pace through the city of New York. By boat, one is introduced first to the Statue of Liberty, beautiful Coney Island, and the landscape with gigantic towers, which proclaim the beginning of a new world after days of seasickness on the Atlantic Ocean. From the beginning the foreigner sees in New York City a micro- or rather macrocosm of the United States, a land of contrasts and extremes, the personification of the dualism characteristic of western life.

Senghor is therefore confronted with this spectacle, which is so unfamiliar to him. Big cities no longer held the wonder they had for him when as a young man, in 1928, he left Dakar on a pilgrimage to Paris. Paris of course is not New York. Despite its population and area, Paris is far from being massive, and the visitor can still see the tops of buildings from the pavements, and more important still, he can look up at the 'Étoile' and the Eiffel Tower without feeling dizzy, without losing his consciousness or his humanity. He can still look at those structures of cement and stone with some admiration for the architect, some feeling for the humanity of the monuments. In New York, the poet Senghor is faced not with historical monuments but with houses where human beings are supposed to live and work, and the feeling is one of misery and dehumanization.

> Et l'angoisse au fond des rues à gratte-ciel
> Levant des yeux de chouette parmi l'éclipse du soleil . . .

> Mais quinze jours sur les trottoirs chauves de Manhattan – C'est au bout de
>   la troisième semaine que vous saisit la fièvre en un bond de jaguar
> Quinze jours sans un puits, ni pâturage, tous les oiseaux de l'air
> Tombant soudain et morts sous les hautes cendres des terrasses.
> Pas un rire d'enfant en fleur, sa main dans ma main fraîche
> Pas un sein maternel, des jambes de nylon. Des jambes et des seins sans
>   sueur ni odeur
> Pas un mot tendre en l'absence de lèvres, rien que des coeurs artificiels
>   payés en monnaie forte
> Et pas un livre où lire la sagesse. La palette du peintre fleurit des cristaux
>   du corail.
> Nuits d'insomnie, ô nuits de Manhattan! si agitées de feux follets, tandis
>   que les klaxons hurlent des heures vides
> Et que les eaux obscures charrient des amours hygiéniques, tels des
>   fleuves en crue des cadavres d'enfants.

[And the disquiet in the depth of your skyscraper streets
Lifting up owl eyes in the sun's eclipse. . . .

But a fortnight on the bald sidewalks of Manhattan – At the end of the third
   week the fever takes you with the pounce of a jaguar
A fortnight with no well or pasture, all the birds of the air
Fall suddenly dead below the high ashes of the terraces.
No child's laughter blossoms, his hand in my fresh hand
No mother's breast. Legs in nylon. Legs and breasts with no sweat and no
   smell.
No tender word for mouths are lipless. Hard cash buys artificial
   hearts.
No book where wisdom is read. The painter's palette flowers with crystals
   of coral.
Insomniac nights O nights of Manhattan, tormented by fatuous fires, while
   the klaxons cry through the empty hours
And dark waters bear away hygienic loves, like the bodies of children on a
   river in flood.]

The child of Joal has arrived in New York. This city is normally baffling for
people from other capitals or big cities in the United States and the rest of the
world. But in New York, this feeling is redoubled for Senghor, who now sees
himself and considers himself not as someone who has lived in Paris but
simply as a black who was born in Joal, a village of Africa. There, in the
villages, man lived in harmony with trees, rivers, animals, gods and the dead
members of the family. Many a time in the poems of Senghor, people, young
and old, sit below the baobab or beneath the kaicedrat and chat, and chat and
chat, or simply doze, and doze and doze. People sit down in the villages. The
old tell stories about age and fairies, the young learn facts about the stars and
life. New York should not be expected to be like Joal, but for the poet, it is
just too different, too inhumanly different to be acceptable or palatable. The
external beauty of New York also masks the immensity of its emptiness. Man
is dehumanized. Nature is denaturized. Things are even 'reified', leaving
nothing but pure matter in place of life itself. A man of flesh and blood disap-
pears in this arid desert overpopulated by creatures filled with anxieties and
worries. It is desert because it lacks the blood that keeps society alive and
together – love. It is nothing but a mass of steel, stones, cement, ivory,
aluminium and corrugated iron sheets. In retrospect, the poet considered
Paris more human, more humane to beings. He must have been thinking of
the Paris he would celebrate during his speech to the Municipal Assembly in
1961, where the 'smile of May and the splendour of September . . . chant the
sweetness of life'. He must have been regretting that Paris, 'a city – a symbol of

stones – looking out on a harmonious countryside of rivers, flowers, forests, hills. A countryside which portrays a soul befitting man. And the whole thing is illuminated by the light of the Spirit.'

New York as seen by Senghor is far from this romanticized Parisian atmosphere. In New York nature is banished, for synthetic products replace natural ones; not only are there artificial orange flavours, synthetic fibres in place of natural cotton, but love and human relations have become synthetic also through the instrument of money and prophylactics. Men, beasts and birds are deprived of their natural habitat. Children are denied a chance to come to being as the rivers and sewage wash away the waste products of hygienic love. Nowhere does one see or feel the smell of humanity. Everywhere is the smell of colognes, perfumes and other artificial odours, disinfectants, pollutants and deodorizers. The poet thinks about his village and the smell of a healthy female after a long day's work in the farm, the healthy smell of sweat and life, the healthy breath of love and nature. This is not possible in New York City with its sky-scrapers, air-conditioned offices, nylon-hosed secretaries and models, perfumed hostesses and stars and over-loving young women – ever ready to embrace anyone at the sight of dollar bills. Their artificial kisses, their artificial smiles, their artificial hearts simulate an artificial love and fashion the artificial cravings of their anxious and worried partners.

In Senghor's New York, remembrance of things past, dreams, reality, and imagination merge together and become inseparable. There is certainly the feeling of alienation. Alienation leads to the reification of an object. This is exactly what Senghor does with New York. Some of his observations are true, but most of them are poetic conceptions of reality, neither true nor false. Senghor knows Paris much better, has come to love that city, and never misses a chance to visit it. In his works he speaks of the city, its monuments, subway stations; Sèvres-Babylone, the parks at Montparnasse, days spent in the Luxembourg Gardens, nights spent carousing in Monmartre. Someone who has lived in New York cherishes memories of the time he spent in the Central Park (however unsafe), in Greenwich Village (hippy though it may be), on Fifth Avenue (crowded, unnatural and treeless as it is). But Senghor is not concerned with urban realities; he is interested in poetic reflections on city life.

The controversial aspect of this poem is when he speaks about Harlem:

Il suffit d'ouvrir les yeux à l'arc-en-ciel d'avril
Et les oreilles, surtout les oreilles à Dieu qui, d'un rire de saxophone, créa
le ciel et la terre en six jours.
Et le septième jour il dormit du grand sommeil nègre.

[It is enough to open your eyes to the April rainbow
And the ears, above all the ears to God who with a burst of saxophone
laughter created the heavens and the earth in six days.
And on the seventh day, he slept his great negro sleep.]

and when he also says:

J'ai vu dans Harlem bourdonnant de bruits de couleurs solennelles et
d'odeurs flamboyantes . . .

Harlem Harlem! Voici ce que J'ai vu. Harlem Harlem! Une brise verte de
blés sourdre des pavés labourés par les pieds nus de danseurs Dans
Groupes ondes de soie et seins de fers de lance, ballets de nénuphars et de
masques fabuleux.

[I have seen Harlem humming with sounds and solemn colour and flam-
boyant smells . . .
Harlem Harlem! I have seen Harlem Harlem! A breeze green with corn
springing from the pavements ploughed by the bare feet of dancers In
Crests and waves of silk and breasts of spearheads, ballets of lilies and
fabulous masks]

He gives the impression that only the black section of New York City, Harlem,
this city within a city, can save the whole. It can save the whole because it is
black and has conserved the properties of African villages. There people, he
believes, are still people with all their frailties, with their rhythm of life, and
with the smell of something, even alcohol. There is still the sound of the
trumpet, the laughter of the saxophone; there are still signs of people sleeping,
this time not beneath baobab trees or kaicedrats but on doorsteps. There are
still signs of life, real human life. There are also signs of people walking
barefoot, unperfumed, unnyloned and ungirded with stockings. While his
observations are poetically true and acceptable, he seems to exhibit the
influence of Arthur de Gobineau, who in 1854 wrote his *Essai sur l'inégalité
des races humaines*, where he spoke about the prodigious endowment of black
people with emotions and artistic prowess, and their almost complete lack of
rational and scientific intelligence or mathematical vision. Senghor, and there
are traces of this in his other works, seems to be giving credance to the
erroneous belief that the blacks alone are endowed with artistic talent, to the
exclusion of other races, a position as false as the theory of Gobineau that
whites and more particularly Germans are endowed with more intelligence than
other peoples. Evident also in Senghor's conception of Harlem is the assigning
of feminine qualities to this section of the city. The white section, lower
Manhattan, appears to possess all the masculine qualities of strength. Harlem

then becomes a living museum of real life in the midst of the artificial museum that is New York. It appears that the black man from Harlem, in spite of centuries of separation from mother Africa, has conserved the qualities that were characteristic of African rural life.

When all is said, the poem is written with a great deal of feeling and sincerity, with deep regret for the absence of rural dimension in New York, and a distant admiration for the modernism of the city. The images are chosen with care, but with ease. It appears that the poem is an accurate photographic image of Senghor's feelings of revolt against and admiration for the city at a particular time and place. No doubt some day in the future he will look back at New York with the same kind of nostalgia and perspective that characterized his vision of Paris in 1961. After all, Paris in 1928 was for him dull and foggy, and in the 1930s it represented racism and oppression. It was that revolt against Paris that gave rise to his emotional longing for Joal and Africa in *Chants d'Ombre*. In the collection *Éthiopiques*, it is the revolt against New York City, against its racism and oppression of the poor and underprivileged, and even oppression of humanity at large, that gives rise to another equally successful poem, 'A New York'. Literature, and poetry in particular, flourishes when there is a conflict of cultures, ideas or beliefs.

By far the most ambitious piece in *Éthiopiques* is the dramatic poem 'Chaka'. According to legend and oral tradition, Chaka was the son of Zulu Chief Senza'Ngakona, and Nandi, whom the chief married when she was already pregnant with Chaka. Because the chief had no other son, he took Chaka as his heir. Soon after, however, his other wives bore him two male children, and under their pressure, the chief had to repudiate Nandi. Thus Chaka, at the same time a bastard and royal son, left the royal home of the father with his mother. Undaunted, and thanks to his keenness and skill, he later received command of the regiments of the sovereign ruler Ding'iswayo. Victim of injustice and the persecution of his relations during infancy, Chaka developed a thirst not only for vengeance but also for domination. This will to dominate became the source of his personality and renown. As architect of his own destiny, Chaka wanted to take his revenge. He conquered and re-organized several ethnic groups and instituted a military system which forbade soldiers in the army to marry. He himself enforced this with his own example by remaining a bachelor. In addition he incorporated within his régime and army the people he conquered. During his reign between 1818 and 1828, he had more than 100,000 soldiers and added more than half a million citizens to his kingdom. His expeditions were usually very bloody, but he was an exceptionally good organizer. He introduced several innovations in African military art, in particular offensive tactics and military organization. But his tragic fault, his thirst for revenge, domination, and by implication blood, led him to the brink of folly, besieged on the one hand by nightmares of his past campaigns and on the other by plots organized by his jealous brothers. These brothers were eventually to kill him, but at the moment of death, he prophesied that after he had gone they would not really be free but would be colonized by the white man, whose subjects and servants his people would become.

Senghor's poem actually begins with the end of the story as written by Thomas Mofolo, at the moment when Chaka's body is pierced by a lance. In the poem there is a mixture of the Greek dramatic use of the choir and the African use of background music. Senghor's poem is far removed from the Chaka of Mofolo, of history, and of legend: far removed from the Zulu hero compared by some to the French soldier Roland in the *Chanson de Roland* and to the Spanish soldier, Cid, in *El Cantar mío Cid*. Senghor's Chaka is no longer the warrior but the moribund. He is no longer the ascetic ruler who encouraged celibacy among his soldiers by setting them an example, but a weak lover of Nolivé, his fiancée whom he loved but avoided. The leader of the nation is forgotten. The only point of resemblance between the Chaka of history and the man painted by Senghor is his assassination by his brothers and his sacrifice of his fiancée, Nolivé.

All through the poem there is dichotomy between Chaka the politician and nationalist and Chaka the individual, who is in love with Nolivé. Some criticis have seen in this a transference of the personal dilemmas the Senegalese poet faced around 1950 as he was confronted with two almost incompatible choices: black nationalism and politics and his growing love for (and eventual marriage to) a white woman. The moral of the tale of the legendary Chaka is that for the sake of the common good, personal love and ambition must be sacrificed. Senghor in his poem, however, was far from implicitly condoning Chaka's murder of thousands of his people for the sake of what he believed was the common good. Chaka loved his people, and in Senghor's poem he is shown as believing that this justifying nationalist principle permitted everything. He was willing to sacrifice everything for the common good.

Certainly the political dimension of Senghor's Chaka should not be ignored in the interpretation of the poem. It is not just a celebration of the Zulu warrior, but should be read in a way as an apology for, or a condemnation of a certain kind of politics. A careful reading of the poem would tend to suggest that all is not permitted in politics, and love of one's people is not enough reason for a dictatorial régime. Chaka, in short, should not have sacrificed his fiancée and his people, even for the good of his nation. Moderation is basic to Senghor's policy and philosophy, and he certainly would disagree with the unsuccessful 1964 American Presidential candidate, Senator Barry Goldwater, who said that 'extremism in the pursuit of liberty is no vice and moderation in the search for justice is no virtue'.

More satisfying poetically, however, is the musical dimension of the work.

In the dramatic poem, Senghor aimed to illustrate what he considered an indigenous form of art where music, painting, theatre, poetry, religion, faith, love and politics are all intertwined. It is basically this music, this poetry and lyricism that turns the entire poem into some kind of a feminine epic poem, that is to say epic in conception, soft and romantic in execution. Senghor's temperament is not geared to epic poetry. That is why in 'Chaka' one hears again the soft, caressing voice of love, subdued after *Chants d'Ombre*. It is not Chaka the soldier whose voice we hear but that of the helpless lover exclaiming 'O ma nuit! ô ma Noire! ma Nolivé!' 'O ma nuit! ô ma blonde! ma lumineuse sur les collines . . . Chair noire de lumière, corps transparent comme au matin du jour premier'. The feminization of Chaka becomes perhaps more comprehensible when the reader considers also the feminization of Harlem and the Congo River elsewhere in Senghor's poetry. Perhaps this is an influence of the matriarchical society of his homeland.

Nocturnes

Nocturnes

▼▼▼▼▼▼▼▼▼▼▼▼▼▼▼▼▼▼▼▼▼▼▼▼▼▼▼▼▼▼▼▼▼

THE VOLUME of poetry entitled *Nocturnes* was published by Léopold Senghor in 1961. But the contents of this volume are not completely new since the two major poems, 'Chants de l'Initié' and 'Chants pour Signare', were already published as far back as 1947 and 1949, the latter as 'Chants pour Naëtt'.

The new pieces in this volume consist of Elegies. In these elegies Senghor tries to put into practice a theory of poetics that he was preaching in the fifties, and which he considers the bedrock of all negro–African poetry.

One of the most fascinating of the elegies is the first one, 'Elégie de Minuit', where the poet, like a painter, plays with shades of light and darkness. Though entitled 'Elégie de Minuit', the poem begins with the brightness of day:

Eté splendide Eté, qui nourris le Poète du lait de ta lumière

[Summer splendid Summer, feeding the Poet with the milk of your light]

The poem is definitely written at night. The poet is reminiscing. Night here has various implications. It is not only the night of day but also towards the night of life. There is a recapitulation of life and age. There is a feeling of nostalgia with the passing of time, of the seasons. The season in question is that of life, and the summer the poet sings is the summer or mid-point of life. The poet is therefore evoking his youth, a fiery youth, full of plans and prospects. It is in this light that one should interpret the next lines:

Moi qui poussais comme blé de Printemps, qui m'enivrais de la verdeur de l'eau, du ruissellement vert dans l'or du Temps

[I grew like corn in the Springtime, I was drunk with verdure of water, with green rustling in the gold of Time]

He is referring here to the spring of life when one grows not only physically but also in ideas, intoxicated as young shoots are by the richness of the water that nourishes the growing fern. That was the golden age when the young man Senghor set out in search of the golden fleece. Thirty years later, as he approaches the ripe age of sixty, the poet can look back at his youth, just in the same way as in *Chants d'Ombre* he looked back from Paris at his childhood.

D

This search into the past is definitely far removed from a similar 'Regret' of François Villon. For Senghor, it is not a past squandered and wasted; it was not a vegetating past but rather a lively one, full of light and the brightness of day, intoxicated not with debilitating alcohol but with stimulating ideas. It is also far removed from an almost similar feeling expressed by Baudelaire in his 'Goût du Néant'. Definitely, as will be pointed out in this poem, Senghor will also thirst for nothingness, for oblivion, but for a different reason. His reason is closer to that of a René Chateaubriand than that of Baudelaire.

Senghor in this poem seems to be gazing directly at the light in front of him. It also looks like a very late night, as he acknowledges:

Ah! plus ne peux supporter ta lumière, la lumière des lampes, ta lumière
  atomique qui disintègre tout mon être
Plus ne peux supporter la lumière de minuit.

[Ah! no longer! I cannot bear your light, the light of your lamps, your
  atomic light breaking up all my being
I cannot bear the light of midnight.]

From a philosophical reflection of the past, he turns sharply to a reflection on the light in front of him as he writes. This steady gaze at an object, any object, in this particular case a lamp, an electric light, makes the object of contemplation look very absurd from the Sartrian point of view. Light becomes nonsensical, and by extension, wisdom becomes absurd, the wisdom accumulated in youth, the wisdom represented by the invention of the electric light, the atomic light that appears to destroy with its rays the being of the poet. A kind of nausea takes hold of him. The light in front of him certainly brings to his mind other lights in other rooms as he toiled all night trying to study, to read, to write. The poet has reached saturation point and does not want to have anything to do with the light. He can no longer bear this brightness in the middle of the night. It is not only the physical brightness that seeks to destroy the tranquillity of the dark night. He also cannot bear the lucidity that comes with reflection and contemplation at night. It brings back old memories, in particular heart-rending ones. It brings back regrets for things past, events that cannot be relived, that cannot be changed.

The tenor of the poem does not really become evident until the next few lines when the poet says:

La splendeur
  des honneurs est comme un Sahara
Un vide immense, sans erg ni hamada, sans herbe, sans un battement de
  cils, sans un battement de coeur.

[The splendour of honours
  is like a Sahara
An immense void, without erg or hamada, without grass, without the flicker
  of an eyelash, or the flicker of a heart.]

The nature of the contemplation becomes clear immediately. The Poet-President seems nauseated by a life filled with political honours and splendour. The statesman seems exhausted with the red-carpet treatment that stands in his way wherever he goes. The light of the day takes another meaning: the bright side of life – success in life. He compares the splendours of office and the honours attached to it to the Sahara Desert, empty and arid. Surrounded certainly by aides-de-camp, ministers, friends, relations and sycophants, the poet still feels alone in the midst of all: hence the reference to the arid feeling, as in a desert. The frustration seems to be akin to that of King Solomon in all his splendour. Nothing under the sun is lasting, and uninterrupted affluence could be boring. The midnight of life is approaching, and like St Augustine, the poet appears to be recognizing that 'our hearts are restless until they rest in [God]'. The emptiness surrounding him can be compared with the dryness and emptiness of New York, whose outside splendour and majesty, as seen already, marks an inner emptiness, a life of worries and anxieties. This is definitely a new dimension in the regrets of the poet from Joal. The emptiness of modern life, of New York City, has now invaded not only Senegal, and his palace, but also his private life.

'Sans un battement de cils' indicates the long nights the President has to endure as he faces one crisis after another in the course of the arduous task of guiding his people. 'Sans un battement de coeur' does not really have its literal sense here. It refers to the absence of real love, the total absence of emotion in political life. Decisions are based not on emotion and the heart but rather on the basis of political expediency, which may often imply the neglect of human considerations. Round the clock, therefore, the mind and the eyes are open, flaming like the lights of a lighthouse to guide the people, all wayfarers in the ship of state. 'Dans mes yeux le phare portugais tourne, oui vingt-quatre heurs sur vingt-quatre. Une mécanique précise et sans répit, jusqu'à la fin des temps.' The poet seems to be revolting against the precision that marks his life and schedule, a stifling kind of mechanical precision.

Senghor in this poem strikes chords that remind the reader of Stéphane Mallarmé, especially the Mallarmé of 'Igitur', 'Un coup de dés n'abolira jamais le hasard' and of the sonnet of the 'Cygne'. There is a feeling of deficiency, absence, drought, void, lack of satisfaction, absence of love, absence of humanity.

There is an implied feeling of inadequacy, of mild disgust. There is the great desire to read and write. But there is also the frustrating feeling of inability to read again, to create again. It is in this vein that one must read the lines:

Je tourne en rond parmi mes livres, qui me regardent du fond de leurs yeux.

[I pace among my books. They gaze at me from the bottom of their eyes.]

The magic powers of vision are transferred to the inanimate cluster of books. It is no longer from the depth of his eyes that the poet watches: rather, the books stare at him from the depth of their wisdom. Across the window, the poet looks at the tropical sky glistening with more than six thousand lamps, the stars of the sky and the lights of the city. The lights give the appearance of luminosity, fairy-like luminosity. Repetition of words and phrases seem to underscore the elegant monotony of this kind of life:

Plus ne peux supporter la lumière, la lumière des lampes ta lumière atomique . . . la lumière de minuit.

Also

Donc vingt-quatre heures sur vingt-quatre, et les yeux grands ouverts comme le Père Cloarec

. . . oui vingt-quatre heures sur vingt-quatre . . .

Six mille lampes qui brûlent vingt-quatre heures sur vingt-quatre.

[So twenty-four hours out of twenty-four, eyes wide open like Father Cloarec

. . . yes twenty-four hours out of twenty-four . . .

Six thousand lamps burning twenty-four hours out of twenty-four.]

The monotony of life, its repetition, its dulling extravagance, has usually one soothing element, one soothing balm – love, which serves as a lubricant for the mechanical piston that is life. But here again, a note of despair is sounded:

Plus ne peut m'apaiser la musique d'amour, le rythme sacré du poème

[I can no longer find peace in the music of love, in the sacred rhythms of the poem.]

The absence of love, or of satisfaction from love, explains the night of insomnia. Unlubricated, the piston of life can no longer move along with ease.

There was a time when politics was a joy for the young poet. In 1945, it was a young idealist that left Senegal to represent his country in Europe:

Ah! de nouveau dormir dans le lit frais de mon enfance
Ah! bordent de nouveau mon sommeil les si chères mains noires
Et de nouveau le blanc sourire de ma mère.
Demain, je reprendrai le chemin de l'Europe, chemin de l'ambassade
Dans le regret du Pays noir.

LE RETOUR DE L'ENFANT PRODIGUE (*Chants d'Ombre*)

[Ah! to sleep once more in the fresh bed of my childhood
Ah! once more those black dear hands to tuck in my sleep
Once more the white smile of my mother.
Tomorrow, I shall take again the road to Europe, road of my embassy
Homesick for my black land.

THE RETURN OF THE PRODIGAL SON (*Chants d'Ombre*)]

In 1956, victory at the polls was celebrated with shouts of joy and chants of glory. A successful and happy deputy set out again to represent his country in Europe. There he was a member of the French Cabinet in the government of Edgar Faure. He was at the European Assembly at Strasbourg. He founded the African Convention. He was very active in politics, being also then a municipal counsellor and the Mayor of Thiès. But after 1960, he attained full political power in Senegal. Disillusionment invaded the heart of the poet. A similar movement had been observed when he was a student in Paris. He had left Senegal in 1928 as an enthusiastic and idealistic young man in search of the golden fleece in Paris. He had struggled very hard, and after an initial failure gained entry into the university, where he worked for his *agrégation*. This objective was attained by 1936. That year also marked the year of the young man's revolt, at least an intellectual revolt against French civilization and European rationalism. In 'Elégie de Minuit', this phenomenon is again recreated in the field of politics. But there is a difference. After the intellectual revolt against French civilization, the poet could still fall back on African civilization, he could still turn to politics for further conquests and successes. There was room at the top and he had places to go to. He was then a young man. But after the revolt against politics evidenced in this poem, there is nothing to fall back on, no place to go to, nothing to aspire to, except perhaps a deep desire for non-being, for oblivion, for nothingness. He is no longer a young man and dusk is fast approaching. This feeling generates the despair that characterizes 'Elégie de Minuit'. Filled perhaps with this realization, the poet continues to fight, and in his mental agony cries:

Contre le désespoir Seigneur, j'ai besoin de toutes mes forces.

[Against despair O Lord, I have need of all my strength.]

There seems to be a return to infancy, a return to God after days, years of errancy, decades of self-sufficiency. The Seminarian turns to prayer and to the Lord for consolation. In this return, he rediscovers the religious cadence of Claudelian poetry, the rhythm, simplicity and spiritualism of Paul Claudel. The despair reminds one of the predicament of Stéphane Mallarmé. But unlike Mallarmé, whose confrontation with inanity, emptiness and despair turns to sterility and contemplation of nothingness, and frigidity before a blank piece of paper, leaving his great work unfinished, Senghor turns to prayer and to God for courage and hope. This will help him at least to escape boredom, even if he does not rediscover happiness:

> Contre le désespoir Seigneur, j'ai besoin de toutes mes forces
> ... Douceur du poignard en plein coeur, jusqu'à la garde
> Comme un remords. Je ne suis pas sûr de mourir.
> Et si c'était cela l'Enfer, l'absence de sommeil ce désert du Poète
> Cette douleur de vivre, ce mourir de ne pas mourir
> L'angoisse des ténèbres, cette passion de mort et de lumière
> Comme les phalènes la nuit sur les lampes-tempêtes, dans l'horrible
> pourrissement des forêts vierges.

> [Against despair O Lord, I have need of all my strength
> ... Sweetness of the dagger full in the heart up to the hilt
> Like remorse. I am not sure to die.
> If that was Hell, the absence of sleep, the desert of the Poet
> The pain of living, dying of not dying
> The agony of darkness, that passion of death and light
> Like moths at night round the storm lamps in the horrible rot of a virgin
> forest.]

There is an irresistible call from the world beyond. The episode looks like a brush with death, and more than a brush, a dialogue with death itself. The scene is a poignant one. It is an intellectual and a philosophical nightmare, and perhaps because of that less frightening and more poetic. The poet appears ready to board another boat, another 'Médie', this time with less enthusiasm, this time bound for the underworld. The fleece this time is not the mastery of French civilization or grammar but a quest for peace in nothingness. He is in search of a *life* that will be *eternal life*, and by implication a *death* that will be real death, the cessation of all anxiety and sorrow. This way alone can he expect to avoid the nightmare, the Hell symbolized by the absence of sleep: 'death that is not really death', a life that is not really life; a life that is full of death and a death that is laden with anxiety. But the predicament of life and death continue to face him as life itself and poetic inspiration dry up, like a virgin forest quickly and horribly losing its virginity and viridity through rot and decrepit age. Immediately the reader realizes that the problem goes beyond mere intellectualization, for the poet himself, in anticipation of the end, real or imagined, writes his epitaph:

Seigneur de la lumière et des ténèbres
Toi seigneur du Cosmos, fais que je repose sous Joal-l'Ombreuse
Que je renaisse au Royaume d'enfance bruissant de rêves
Que je sois le berger de ma bergère par les tanns de Dyilôr où fleurissent les
  Morts
Que j'éclate en applaudissements quand entrent dans le cercle Téning-
  N'dyaré et Tyagoum-N'dyaré
Que je danse comme l'Athlète au tamtam des Morts de l'année.
Ce n'est qu'une prière. Vous savez ma patience paysanne.
Viendra la paix viendra l'Ange de l'aube, viendra le chant des oiseaux
  inouïs
Viendra la lumière de l'aube.
Je dormirai du sommeil de la Mort qui nourrit le Poète – O Toi qui donnes
  la maladie du sommeil aux nouveaux nés, à Marone la Poétesse à Kotye-
  Barma le Juste! . . .
Je dormirai à l'aube, ma poupée rose dans les bras
Ma poupée aux yeux vert et or, à la langue si merveilleuse
La langue même du poème.

[Lord of the light and the darkness
Thou Lord of the Cosmos let me rest under the shade of Joal
Let me be born again into the Kingdom of childhood alive with rustling
  dreams
Let me be the shepherd to my shepherdess among the sea-flats of Dyilor
  where the dead prosper
Let me burst into clapping when Tening-N'dyaré and Tyagum-Ndyaré
  enter the circle
Let me dance like the Athlete to the drum of the year's Dead.
All this is only a prayer. You know my peasant patience.
Peace will come, the Angel of Dawn will come, the song of the preposterous
  birds will come
The light of the dawn will come.
I shall sleep the sleep of death by which the Poet is fed
(O Thou who givest sleeping sickness to newborn babies, to Marone the
  Poetess, to Kotye-Barma the Just!)
I shall sleep at dawn, my pink doll in my arms
My doll with green eyes and golden, and so wonderful a tongue
Being the tongue of the poem.]

The end has come. This is the Senghorian adieu to poetry, to literature, to life. The poet may write other poems, the President may serve other terms before his real retirement, but this should be considered his epilogue to life, to poetry. Any serious edition of his work, if it is to be logical, should have 'Elégie de Minuit' as the poet's 'last' poem.

Life has come full circle. His style has come full circle as well. Life that started at Joal-L'Ombreuse is about to repose in the same paternal land, where the poet hopes to be reincarnated. Like Chateaubriand, who wanted to be buried at Combourg, like Ronsard, who also wrote a poem 'De l'élection de son sépulcre', Senghor here is seeking a final resting-place. The choice is logical. Joal is the land of childlike dreams, the land that haunted the student in times of success and failure in Paris, the village that haunted the President in times of splendour and misery in Dakar. It is not just Joal that he desires, but a certain kind of Joal, the one he knew as a child. That Joal will not exist again, and perhaps never existed except in the mind of the poet. It is the Joal of childhood before the age of seven. It is Joal where the living and the dead communicate, the Joal of Marone, chanting the praises of the living and the admonitions of the dead. It is the Joal of the precious fears of childhood that the poet spoke about in his 'Post-face' to *Éthiopiques*. That Joal never really existed in time and space. Its existence lies beyond the realms of time and space, beyond the span of life and death. The Joal of Senghor existed, exists and will perpetually exist in Senghor's poetry, in Senghor's *Chants d'Ombre*.

It may be because of this that this poem (as indicated earlier, his style has come full circle) recaptures the infancy, simplicity, nostalgia, reverie, emotion and cadence of the poems of *Chants d'Ombre*. Joal is revisited at the midnight of life, before the zero hour of existence. The poet desires a homecoming, a return to quiet and simple life. He left Joal, the land of native wisdom, in pursuit of technical knowledge. He left Joal, where he was heir to father's land and titles, in search of the power of national politics. As the midnight of life approaches, at least poetically, there is a regret for the years spent in pursuit of artificial knowledge, artificial power. As his final wish, the poet would want to be reborn in Joal, a shepherd married to a shepherdess and living peacefully the life of a villager, among his people, dead and living, a lord to no man and a slave to no one. He would like to find his joys and amusement in the village where every year he can dance, without monotony, like the athlete in commemoration of the year's dead.

The poem ends on a note of tranquillity, the peace of death. Peace will come, likewise the Angel of dawn, because death, the midnight or zero hour of life, is only a dawn or birth into a new world. As is normal on such occasions, people will see and hear omens announcing the demise of one of their kind, such as strange birds intoning their laments to warn of the departure of a native son. The final moment, which is not really final, being the beginning of a new life, will be 'la lumière de l'aube' – a dawn into a new life. But as that dawn approaches, poetically at least, there is a remembrance of the loved ones being left behind, 'ma poupée rose . . . aux yeux vert et or'. The poet wants to cling to them, cling to life and Joal a little longer. Certainly, the dead, according to Serere metaphysics, are ever present among the living. But it is a different kind of presence, a life that is not really life, death that is not really death. Hence the dilemmas of life are not even solved in death. So even if, buried in Joal after death, the poet could write from the other world, speak or express himself, there is reason to believe that there would still be that nostalgic remembrance of Joal-L'Ombreuse, a nostalgic recreation of the life that is no more.

In general, reactions to Senghor's publication of *Nocturnes* were mixed. Some people saw it as the end of the ambivalence that had characterized Senghor's poetry. They saw the earlier conflict between African and European culture calming down, with the poet fully reconciled to his African heritage and expressing himself with a unity of purpose.

Senghorian Aesthetics

Senghorian Aesthetics

▼▼▼▼▼▼▼▼▼▼▼▼▼▼▼▼▼▼▼▼▼▼▼▼▼▼▼▼▼▼▼▼▼▼

PERHAPS AS important, in a way, as Senghor's poetry is his philosophy of African art. His earlier poetry partly gave rise to this philosophy as such as this philosophy later dominated and informed his later works. Senghor has basically an essentialist conception of life and art. He read the works of Arthur de Gobineau and Gustave Le Bon and Élie Faure. As a result of a variety of influences, Senghor came to the conclusion, like several intellectuals of his time and day, that the blacks were beings exceptionally endowed with artistic genius, and this to the exclusion of other qualities. This led him to propounding such erroneous doctrines as 'reason is European as emotion is negro', and stating that blacks do not have the intelligence to pursue mathematical and scientific studies.

Some of these ideas came from the works of Arthur de Gobineau, especially *Essai sur l'inégalité des races humaines* (1853), where Gobineau divided the human race into white, yellow and black types. The negro of Gobineau is simply a being of desire and emotion. The racism and exaggeration implicit in Gobineau's ideas are self-evident, and Senghor's mistake was to read Gobineau without due judgement and critical appraisal.

In Gobineau's scheme the whites, as opposed to the blacks, possess reflective energy and energetic intelligence, and the notion of the useful, from an elevated point of view, implying courage and idealism. These qualities, according to him, are not possessed by the black and the yellow races.

Whites, according to Gobineau, possess a determination and perseverance that know how to skilfully face and surmount obstacles. Whites stand for order, have a developed sense of thirst for liberty. Whites, according to Gobineau, not only show a marked hatred of the formalist organization responsible for the somnolence of the Chinese, but equally disdain the haughty despotism which constitutes the only rein capable of restraining black people. Within this Gobinesque philosophy, the animality of the negro is opposed by the rationality of the whites, and on the basis of this fundamental thesis (or racial prejudice) actions and reactions by blacks and whites are diversely interpreted by him. For example, whites attach a great price to human life, but, says Gobineau, they would not hesitate to commit suicide for honour or for a higher goal. Being rational beings, whites are conscious when they are cruel. The blacks, according to Gobineau, do not value life and do not hesitate to kill others or kill themselves for trifles.

Nevertheless, Gobineau was one of the first to underscore the artistic endownment of the negro, though his analysis of this phenomenon was falsified by the prejudices of his time. Thus he wrote:

> Yes, again, the negro is the human being that is the most powerfully gripped by the artistic instinct, on the essential condition however that his intellect has grasped the sense and understood the meaning of the subject. For if you show him the Juno of Polyclitus, it is doubtful whether he will appreciate it. He doesn't know who Juno is, and this likeness in marble intended to convey certain transcendental ideas of the beautiful which are as yet quite unknown to him, will leave him as cold as the statement of an algebraic problem. In the same way, if one were to translate lines from the *Odyssey*, for example the meeting of Ulysses with Nausicaa, the peak of well-considered inspiration: he will go to sleep. With all beings, for a sympathetic chord to be struck, the intellect must first have understood, and there is the difficulty with the negro, whose mind is obtuse, incapable of rising above the lowest level, from the moment when he has to consider, learn, compare, draw inferences.
>
> The artistic sensitivity of this being, in itself inexpressible powerful, will therefore necessarily remain confined to the most wretched occupations. It will be excited and impassioned, but to what end? For the sake of ludicrous, crudely coloured images. It trembles with adoration before a hideous tree-trunk, more moved, a thousand times more possessed by this degrading spectacle than the noble soul of Pericles ever was at the feet of Olympian Jupiter. You see, the negro can raise his mind as far as the ludicrous image, as far as the hideous piece of wood, but when he encounters true beauty, this mind is genetically deaf, dumb and blind.[1]

One cannot ignore the blind and erroneous judgement passed here by Gobineau. Perhaps it is doubtful whether the black man is able to admire the Juno of Polyclitus, but it is certain that Gobineau has shown himself totally incapable of appreciating the transcendental beauty represented by the sculpture in wood of the African deities, like the *Amadioha* of the Ibos, for instance. He has demonstrated a ridiculous lack of intelligence in his failure to understand forms of art and expression not based on Graeco-Roman concepts.

It appears therefore that Senghor during his stay in Paris was attracted to the Gobineau that was institutionalizing the prodigious ability of the negro in the field of artistic creation. This discovery was further reinforced by

[1] Vol. II, pp. 92–4.

ethnological and anthropological revelations by scholars like Frobenius, Delafosse, Ortiz, and Labouret. Senghor could therefore say in 'Négritude et Marxisme' (*Pierre Teilhard de Chardin et la politique africaine*, 1962):

> We rediscovered our pride. Calling attention to the works of anthropologists, prehistorians and ethnologists – paradoxically white – we proclaimed ourselves, with the poet Aimé Césaire, the 'Elder Children of the Earth'. Did we not dominate the world up to Neolithic times, fertilize the civilizations of the Nile and Euphrates before they later became the innocent victims of white barbarians, nomadic tribes descending from their Euro-asiatic plateaus? I must confess, our pride was fast turning into racism.

Gobineau, as has been pointed out, was among the first to recognize the artistic endowment of blacks, and Senghor, it appears, closed his eyes to the racist aspects of Gobineau's philosophy. Below is a schematic summary of the main points made by Gobineau and Le Bon in differentiating the whites and the blacks:

GOBINEAU

BLACK RACE	WHITE RACE
A grossly powerful physical energy	Spiritual and reflective energy
Mediocre thinking faculties	Energetic intelligence; superior intelligence
A will of powerful intensity	Perseverance that is aware of difficulties and finds ways and means of solving them
A bundle of desires and emotions	Inferiority in the intensity of his feelings
Highly developed sense of taste and smell	
Gluttonous, unstable of humour, a human machine	Love and thirst for liberty
Kills wilfully; lazy and imperturbable	Instinct for law and order
Lyrical poet, musician, sculptor	Special love for life, high sense of honour

GUSTAVE LE BON

[Author of *Les lois psychologiques de l'évolution des peuples* (1896): promulgated ideas similar to those of Gobineau]

Incapacity to reason, to compare	A great ability to draw analogies and conclusions from ideas
Inability to perceive analogies and differences	A highly developed critical spirit and precision in judgement
A great credulity and a great absence of critical judgement	Understands the importance of discipline, and the necessity of sacrificing himself to an ideal
Inability to dominate his reflex impulses	

Senghor certainly read the ideas of Gobineau with great interest, and echoes of Gobineau fill his works. In 1937 in Dakar he declared: 'You see, one should not misunderstand or force one's endowments, especially when the heart and mind are involved. We could never beat European peoples in mathematics, exceptional men apart, which would confirm that we are not a race endowed with abstract qualities.' In the same speech in Dakar he continued: 'To be more specific, I have the impression that the natives of French West Africa, exceptions apart, are more gifted in the Letters than in the Sciences; I am afraid that these openings are not being made easy for those interested in literature, though we should regard our scientists with special love because they are rare.' Two years later, Senghor would say that 'emotion is negro, as reason is hellenic'. Elsewhere, following the motto of René Descartes, 'Cogito, ergo sum' – (I think, therefore I am) Senghor would give his version of this in the light of the negro's endowments: 'I feel, therefore I am.' In the same vein is his assertion that European reason is analytical through utilization while negro reason is intuitive through participation. Underscoring this view he also wrote:

I have often written that *emotion is negro*. I have been reproved for this. Wrongly. I don't see how else to account for our specific quality, that *negritude* which is 'the sum total of the cultural values of the black world'.[2]

Senghor's ideas could be summarized in this fashion:

[2] 'Eléments constitutifs d'une civilisation d'inspiration négro-africaine', *Liberté I : Négritude et humanisme*, Paris, Seuil, 1964, p. 250.

LÉOPOLD SÉDAR SENGHOR

BLACK RACE	WHITE RACE
Energetically overtaken by emotion	Reason is hellenic
Emotion is negro	Discursive reason
Great emotional warmth, storm-like vitality	
Intuition: intuitive reason through participation	Analytical reason through utilization
Literature and arts	Mathematics and the sciences
Dance and music	
Race of concrete conceptions	An abstract race
Tendency towards anthropomorphism	
Subjectivism	Objectivity in thought, conceptions
Violence is part of its essence	
Inability to conceive objects in their essence	
I feel, therefore I am	I think, therefore I am

One also sees the influence of Gobineau on Senghor's philosophy, in particular in the latter's conception of *métissage culturel,* the symbiotic mixture not only of cultures but also of races. Gobineau seems to dwell on the evil side of this mixing. For Gobineau this implies the gradual bastardization of the pure and superior white race. Senghor sees only a symbiotic union where blacks will bring to the rendezvous of the races their special musical, artistic and dancing talents. With Senghor, the Gobineau theory of *métissage culturel* is purified of its racism. This is part and parcel of the Senghorian poetic vision, which is basically optimistic. Gobineau is not optimistic. Some young blacks, moved by a feeling of racial pride, sometimes see in Senghor's doctrine of racial mixing and intermarriage an intellectual justification of his private acts. (In 1956 Senghor divorced his black wife to marry a white French secretary and friend of the former wife.) This doctrine of the mixing of the races was later to influence his changing conception of negritude. Some young Africans react against this doctrine, which seems to accept the prejudiced thesis of Gobineau on the subject of the black races.

In the final analysis, reason is as much black as it is hellenic. Emotion, too, is present in both whites and blacks. Blacks may possess exceptional qualities in the area of dance, music and the arts, but to term these the only and exclusive endowments of the negro is, at the least, misleading. If there is any race that exclusively possesses dance, music and the arts, it is certainly not the black, white, yellow, or brown race, but rather the *human race* in all its colours, in all its ramifications, though certain countries may be more advanced from the technological point of view (and this has nothing to do with race), while others still remain closely attached to their ancestral values and customs.

Another important element or ingredient in the formation of Senghorian aesthetics is the surrealist movement, which was current in Europe during Senghor's formative years. The surrealist doctrine, in a way, led him to the recognition of certain exceptional qualities of black African art. After the First World War, Europe suffered from a serious crisis of confidence. Science and rational knowledge had failed to prevent a world war, in fact had made it more devastating. Science had also failed to give a sense of being to man. The writings of Freud in the field of psychology had suggested the power of the animal and hidden impulses in man. The surrealist group of writers, headed by André Breton, who in 1924 wrote the first *Manifeste du Surréalisme*, were out to fight against the form man had imposed upon traditional life. It is understandable that Senghor and his friends, in particular Aimé Césaire, should use the techniques of surrealism in their fight against white racism and European colonialism, both of which were forms that European man had imposed on traditional African life. Even more important still, surrealism, which was moving away from the excessive control of life by science, adopted several creative techniques common in traditional African societies, and for that matter in all societies retaining their traditional and agrarian roots.

The European, in order to rediscover this land of dreams and fantasy, had to go back to European medieval lore, or during the Romantic period, prompted by the archaeological discoveries of the time, to Oriental life. After the excesses of the Romantic era, the medieval period lost some of its charm, and after the nineteenth century the Orient, often visited and revisited in literature, lost some of its mystery. So with the arrival of Freud on the psychological scene, a new source for wonders and fantasy had to be found: the latent and hidden energies of man, his subconscious, the obscure regions of his psyche, the real sources of imagination, fantasy and desire. This was basically the surrealist method.

Senghor saw in this technique the traditional mode of thought of the peasant in an African village. For him, therefore, surrealism was like a christening or baptism of the traditional African way of life. The African does not need

Freud to reveal to him the world of the subconscious, of wonder, of fantasy. It is interesting to note that ethnologists of that particular period propagated the theory that the African had no subconscious, reality and dream being coexistential co-ordinates of his life. Senghor in his writings was also to affirm this absence of division between life and death, dream and reality in traditional African life. Surrealism served to resolve an important complex in the life of Senghor at this particular period. By adopting the surrealist techniques, he was at the same time modern and African: educated and modernist from the white European viewpoint, traditional and faithful to the motherland from the African viewpoint. This dualism, or rather ambivalence, is ever present in Senghor's theories, poetry and actions.

So what the surrealists sought to achieve through the subconscious and psychoanalysis, Senghor believed he could realize by simply returning to African sources. Thus Senghor tried to obtain by an intellectual return to Joal, to his infancy, to traditional and peasant Africa, what Breton and other surrealists sought to obtain in dreams, or what a psychoanalyst of the Freudian era would seek to get from his patient lying down on the couch – a non-logical and non-rational monologue; a chant and flow of thought unguided by critical reason; or in the case of the African village cantor, a chant inspired by the spirit, over which the cantor has no control, being merely a medium used by the gods to sing the praises of the dead, to admonish the living, warn the wicked, forecast the future, foretell times of pestilence, famine, tragedy, and death, and even predict the sex of the unborn child. The surrealist is from this point of view like a village cantor, who improvises, in a spasm of psychic automatism, guided by an internal or extrasensory rhythm and music and the exigencies of the moment, mood and emotion, speaking of death, accident, the birth of a child, return of a prodigal son, pestilence, or even the flash of an idea, no matter how incongruous.

Returning to these integral parts of traditional African culture, Senghor was able to articulate an aesthetics of negro-African art akin to surrealism, except that what was natural to the African cantor (the *griot* in Senegal and in Igboland *onye-amuma* or *onye-ntu*) involved a conscious effort or an artificial genesis in the case of the European surrealist poet.

Besides the metaphysical aspect of Senghor's aesthetics, there are his equally cogent observations on African art, especially with respect to the unity of African art-forms. Olaudah Equiano, Gustavus Vassa, an Igbo man captured by slave traders, had made similar observations about Igbo culture in his book *The Interesting Narrative of the Life of Olaudah Equiano, or Gustavsus Vassa the African, written by himself* (1789): 'We are a nation of dancers, musicians, and poets. Thus every great event such as a triumphant return from battle or other cause of public rejoicing is celebrated in public dances which are accompanied with songs and music suited to the occasion.'

Senghor in his analysis of Serere tradition also emphasized that Serere song, poetry and music were akin to those of the Greek odes. Senghor did not merely write about this phenomenon. He tried, with varying degrees of success, to make practical use of the techniques he observed. Quite a few of his poems have indications as to the kind of musical instruments that should be played with the poems. He gave a double explanation of this attempt to merge music, dance and poetry. Firstly, he sees the musical instruments as giving a sonorous background to the poem, expressing its feeling, colour and tone. The African poem, secondly, is not only music, it is dance at the same time. Some of the instruments suggested by Senghor include the *kora*, long and short tomtoms, drums, xylophones and African violas. It is interesting to note that Langston Hughes and Ramon Guirao also used such indications in their poems, and Senghor was familiar with these by 1936, when he himself was beginning to write in this genre.

In the first collection of his poems, *Chants d'Ombre*, the music is internal, not external. We hear the rhapsody of the griots during the funeral celebrations. 'Pagan' voices rhythmically chant the Christian *Tantum Ergo*. Choristers encourage wrestling and competing champions with their songs. We hear the night chants of mediums. Even in Europe, we hear the sobbing throb of jazz music, the lonely notes of blues rhythm. There is also the rhythm of the machine, the rhythm of prayer, the rhythm of love, the rhythm of life.

The process is intensified in *Hosties noires*, his second volume. There the *kora* and the *tama* are the important musical instruments used. But in *Éthiopiques* musical indications become the rule, not the exception. The poem on the Congo River is accompanied by three *koras* and a xylophone. 'A New York' is written for a full jazz orchestra, a solo trumpet and an oboe. *Chants d'Ombre*, as the name indicates, contains fireside songs and poems. *Hosties noires* is a series of dirges and war songs, exhortatory and lamentatory. *Éthiopiques* contains political songs about Africa, the land of 'Ethiopia'. *Nocturnes* suggests night-time songs, and in fact contains 'Chants pour Signare', 'Chants de l'Initié' and 'Elégies'.

Senghor also makes a very serious and sometimes successful effort to add dramatic dimension to his poems. This is particularly the case with 'Chaka'. The dramatic intent and musical effects have created beautiful lyrical poem, but have done less than justice to Chaka the leader, the hero and warrior. Chaka's history is more tragic than comical, and love is an incidental element in his life. In wishing to make it a tragi-comedy in the fashion of *Romeo and Juliet*, the poet was undertaking the difficult task of turning a historical tragedy of epic dimensions into a light musical drama.

Conclusion

Conclusion

▼▼▼▼▼▼▼▼▼▼▼▼▼▼▼▼▼▼▼▼▼▼▼▼▼▼▼▼▼▼▼▼▼▼

OUR ANALYSIS of Senghor's work started with an examination of his predecessors and their influence, if any, on him and on the development of his ideas and theories. It would be interesting to end this essay with a note on the impact of Senghor on the poetic tradition in African literature, and Senghor's influence on younger African writers, poets in particular. The influence of Senghor, direct or indirect, has gone far beyond the francophone world. He is certainly one of the greatest poets of contemporary Africa. He was one of the propagandists of negritude, which inspired some and alienated others, and was also the source of the rise and fall of many. Senghor sees negritude as the quality or essence of being negro or black, the specific property of the negro-African. Within this essentialist framework, the African can and should only write in a given way, the *negritude* way, if he is really to express his Africanness.

This 'negritude', involving a cultural re-evaluation of black African civilization, is similar, though different in emphasis, to what anglophone leaders at the beginning of the sixties referred to as the 'African personality'. Language does not always express human thought very successfully. While it is admissible that there are essential elements in black African civilizations, it would be futile to try to create a totalist or absolutist African cultural value like *negritude* or *Muntu* in the sense of a racial or continental *Veltanschauung* or world-view. Certain trends run through African societies, and some of these I have pointed out here and elsewhere. It is unacceptable to try to impose structures or values on a people, still less on a race, or to expect all writers to write in a certain way.

The 'negritude' way should therefore not be the only way of writing in Africa. In fact, in view of linguistic differences, both African and European, one would still have to speak in terms of African literatures and not African literature. In traditional society, literature had much in common all over Africa, as with all literatures of the oral tradition. With the impact of colonialism there came divergence, but as long as colonial literature was primarily a revolt against the other, the expatriate oppressor, African colonial literature, especially its poetry, had much in common. But there were differences, with francophone writers emphasizing cultural emancipation, anglophone writers of West Africa proclaiming political freedom, and black writers of southern Africa preaching racial pride. With independence, at least some measure of national independence, literature became nationalized as well, though certain general continental currents prevailed. The experiences of Ghanaians were different from those of the Senegalese and the Nigerians. These experiences influenced the development of the literatures. Furthermore, there are distinct periods within the literatures of various nations. To mention two examples, the highly idealistic, nationalist and pan-African literature of Nkrumah's Ghana is radically different from the decadent realism and self-criticism manifest in the literature of post-Nkrumah Ghana. In Nigeria, literature within that country as a whole was never really homogeneous. After the Nigeria–Biafra war, since the war experiences of Biafrans and other Nigerians were not the same in spite of unification, divergent views of the reality of the Nigerian experience will for a long time to come modify the Nigerians' vision of the world, and consequently the literature emanating from Igboland[1] and the rest of Nigeria.

Thus the absolutist aspects of negritude should be viewed with a very critical eye. It is wrong however to discredit the whole idea of negritude. It should be seen in the context of evolution in literature. Senghor is as wrong in wanting to impose negritude forever on African writers as Wole Soyinka of Nigeria is in challenging the Senegalese writer by saying that a 'tiger does not speak of its tigritude'. The black man at the beginning of the century, and more so around 1936, had to shout about his blackness, not only because of the white racism that had dominated western culture for more than three thousand years, but also because of the racism and fascism ravaging Europe in the 1930s. To defend himself, the black writer, to use the words of Jean-Paul Sartre, had to adopt intellectual militancy, positing in antithesis an anti-racist black racism to combat the thesis of white supremacy and racism, which was then both overt and implicit in the world in various forms, either through cultural domination (in language and religion) or through political subjugation (in the form of slavery and colonialism).

Senghor rejects this negative definition of negritude, but nevertheless it has an existential validity. The whole purpose of negritude, within the Sartrian perspective, was to draw attention to and eventually destroy white racism. But in destroying racism it will destroy its 'racist' self, outlive its usefulness, giving way to humanism in literature. Though Frantz Fanon, who incidentally is critical of negritude, accuses Sartre of destroying negritude before its birth by his use of European dialectics, Sartre's analysis (and this was all he attempted) is worthy of note. Negritude should therefore be seen as a stage in the evolution of the literature of the black man. It *was* necessary, then, for the tiger to speak about his tigritude. Wole Soyinka is partly right, however, if he means that the black writer of today no longer needs to shout from roof-tops that black is beautiful. Not because the Sartrian synthesis of non-racial world

[1] Europeans say 'Ibo' but the correct word is 'Igbo'.

humanism has been achieved, or will of necessity be achieved, but rather because the world has now accepted, if not the *beauty* of blacks, at least their dark presence in the literary world. The contemporary trend in African poetry seems to be away from the negritude movement as the racism and colonialism that inspired this literature dies out or becomes less barefaced. The African poet of today is becoming introspective and personal, almost romantic again. But this is a natural reaction to two or three decades of the poetry of revolt.

Finally, a poet is first and foremost an individual before he is an African. A poet first expresses himself before he thinks of expressing, if he does at all, the psyche of his people. His works should be read with this in mind. Studies of the work of Senghor have generally neglected the individual side of his art. To the mind of the uninitiated, his name evokes the doctrine of negritude, racial literature, the advocacy of black values, a reversal of the colonial literary order and the re-evaluation of African civilization. This over-socio-logical vision loses sight of the man and the individual: the identification of the individual with the race becomes total and, for the critic, Senghor's aesthetics become those of negro-Africa; the crises in the life of the man take on the dimensions of racial complexes. Such an approach seems partial and insufficient. The aim of this study has been: (*a*) to place Léopold Senghor in the general context of the awakening black man and the Black Renaissance in the twentieth century, and especially in the context of the black man's poetry during this period; (*b*) to attempt to understand Senghor's poetry as much as an expression of his inner being as a chronicle of the various moments of his existence, his hopes and his successes, his aims and how they are realized; (*c*) to try, finally, to examine Senghor's aesthetics in order to show what trends have influenced its formation and development, and to what extent the poet has remained faithful to his theory of art.

All the important elements of Senghor's life have been taken into considera-tion: his family, his village, his tribe, his country, and the world at the time of his upbringing and artistic development. The geography and the traditional beliefs of the environment which produced the poet have not been forgotten; his French education, religious and classical background, and the probable influence of these factors on his life and work have been examined. The hopes of the child and his disappointments have been taken into account, as well as the youthful ambitions and achievements of the adult. The analysis however sought to go beyond the sociological by reintegrating these findings into the framework of the life and work of Senghor considered as a whole. We have tried to understand the man better: the poet through the politician, the lover through the poet, and vice versa. All these separate aspects of the individual play their respective roles in forging the man's total personality.

It would appear from this that Senghor's contribution to the defence and embellishment of black civilization rests primarily on his aesthetics and his humanism. One sees too that Senghor, whether or not he is overtaken by events, has already left his mark on negro-African literature. But it is difficult to predict whether Senghor's poetry will excite the same approbation when the prestige of the President and that of the ideologist no longer colour people's view of the man. In spite of the fervid reactions of some black writers of the new generation against Senghor's essentialist view of the black man, the Senegalese poet will certainly survive in the history of the Black Renaissance as the ideologist and theoretician of negritude, which according to him represents 'all the cultural values of black people'.

Bibliographical Note

▼▼▼▼▼▼▼▼▼▼▼▼▼▼▼▼▼▼▼▼▼▼▼▼▼▼▼▼▼▼▼▼

For a more detailed analysis of the work of Senghor and the various factors that seem to have influenced his writings, readers may like to consult my study in French: *Léopold Sédar Senghor et la défense et illustration de la civilisation noire*, 232 pp. (Éditions Marcel Didier, Paris, 1968). The work in question also has an extensive bibliography of the writings of Senghor, of reviews of his works, articles on him and works about the Black Renaissance in general (pp. 207–32). Readers also should consult Senghor's book: *Liberté I: négritude et humanisme*, 445 pp. (Editions du Seuil, Paris, 1964), which is a compilation of the poet's essays and speeches on various aspects of black civilization and writing. There is of course no substitute for the poet's complete works: *Poèmes* (including *Chants d'Ombre*, *Hosties Noires*, *Éthiopiques*, *Nocturnes*, and *Poèmes divers*), 256 pp. (Editions du Seuil, Paris, 1964). *Nocturnes* is also available in the African Writers Series, 64 pp. (Heinemann Educational Books, London, 1970). Below is a short list of other works the reader may find helpful.

ANTHOLOGIES AND SELECTIONS

Armand Guibert, *Léopold Sédar Senghor*, 215 pp. (Éditions Pierre Seghers, Paris, 1961).

Armard Guibert, *Léopold Sédar Senghor*, 175 pp. (Présence Africaine, Paris, 1962).

John Reed and Clive Wake, *Selected Poems*, 99 pp. (Atheneum Press, New York, Oxford University Press, London, 1964).

John Reed and Clive Wake, *Senghor: Prose and Poetry*, 190 pp. (Oxford University Press, London, 1965).

John Reed and Clive Wake, *A Book of African Verse*, 128 pp. (Heinemann Educational Books, London, 1964).

John Reed and Clive Wake, *French African Verse with English translation*, 192 pp. Heinemann Educational Books, London, 1972).

ARTICLES AND BOOKS

Mustapha Bal, 'L'Homme noir dans la poésie', *Pensée* No. 103, May–June 1962, pp. 18–29.

Georges Balandier, 'La littérature noire de langue française', *Présence Africaine* Nos. 8–9, 1950, pp. 393–402.

Naomi M. Garret, 'French Poets of African Descent', *College Language Association Journal*, vol. V, 1961, pp. 41–53.

Abiola Irele, 'Negritude – Literature and Ideology', *Journal of Modern African Studies*, No. 3, Vol. 4, 1964, pp. 499–526.

Irene Dobbs Jackson, 'Negritude in Full Bloom: A Study in Outline', *College Language Association Journal*, VII, No. I, September 1963, pp. 77–83.

Edward Allen Jones, 'Diallo and Senghor as Interpreters of the new French Africa', *French Review*, No. 20, May 1948, pp. 444–9; 'Senghor, voix de l'Afrique noire', *College Language Association Journal*, vol. VIII, No. 2, December 1964, pp. 121–31.

Lilyan Kesteloot, *Les écrivains noirs de langue française: naissance d'une littérature*, 344 pp. (Institut de Sociologie de l'Université Libre de Bruxelles, 1965), in particular pp. 175–201.

S. Okechukwu Mezu, 'Poetry and Revolution in Modern Africa', *The Tropical Dawn* (Black Academy Press, Buffalo 1970) pp. 7–24; (ed.) *Modern Black Literature*, 192 pp. (Black Academy Press, Buffalo, 1971) 192 pp.

Gerald Moore, 'Léopold Sédar Senghor: Assimilation or Negritude', *Seven African Writers* (Oxford University Press, London, 1962) pp. 1–17.

Index

▼▼▼▼▼▼▼▼▼▼▼▼▼▼▼▼▼▼▼▼▼▼▼▼▼▼▼▼▼▼▼▼▼▼▼▼▼▼